104 great discussion starters for youth groups

MIKE YACONELLI & SCOTT KOENIGSAECKER

Youth Specialties

GRAND RAPIDS, MICHIGAN 49530

ISBN 0-310-52501-2

Edited by J. Cheri McLaughlin
Interior design by JamisonBell Advertising and Design
Cover design by Michael Kern Design
Cover photo by Rob Gage—FPG International

Printed in the United States of America

01 02 03 04 05 06 07 08 /CH/ 25 24 23 22 21 20 19 18 17 16 15

Resources from Youth Specialties

Youth Ministry Programming

Camps, Retreats, Missions, & Service Ideas (Ideas Library)
Compassionate Kids: Practical Ways to Involve Your Students in Mission and Service
Creative Bible Lessons from the Old Testament
Creative Bible Lessons in 1 & 2 Corinthians
Creative Bible Lessons in Galatians and Philippians
Creative Bible Lessons in John: Encounters with Jesus
Creative Bible Lessons in Romans: Faith on Fire!
Creative Bible Lessons on the Life of Christ
Creative Bible Lessons in Psalms
Creative Junior High Programs from A to Z, Vol. 1 (A-M)
Creative Junior High Programs from A to Z, Vol. 2 (N-Z)
Creative Meetings, Bible Lessons, & Worship Ideas (Ideas Library)
Crowd Breakers & Mixers (Ideas Library)
Downloading the Bible Leader's Guide
Drama, Skits, & Sketches (Ideas Library)
Drama, Skits, & Sketches 2 (Ideas Library)
Drama, Skits, & Sketches 3 (Ideas Library)
Dramatic Pauses
Everyday Object Lessons
Games (Ideas Library)
Games 2 (Ideas Library)
Games 3 (Ideas Library)
Good Sex: A Whole-Person Approach to Teenage Sexuality & God
Great Fundraising Ideas for Youth Groups
More Great Fundraising Ideas for Youth Groups
Great Retreats for Youth Groups
Holiday Ideas (Ideas Library)
Hot Illustrations CD-ROM
Hot Illustrations for Youth Talks
Hot Illustrations for Youth Talks 4
More Hot Illustrations for Youth Talks
Still More Hot Illustrations for Youth Talks
Ideas Library on CD-ROM
Incredible Questionnaires for Youth Ministry
Junior High Game Nights
More Junior High Game Nights
Kickstarters: 101 Ingenious Intros to Just about Any Bible Lesson
Live the Life! Student Evangelism Training Kit
Memory Makers
The Next Level Leader's Guide
Play It! Over 150 Great Games for Youth Groups
Roaring Lambs
Screen Play
So What Am I Gonna Do With My Life?
Special Events (Ideas Library)
Spontaneous Melodramas
Spontaneous Melodramas 2
Student Leadership Training Manual
Student Underground: An Event Curriculum on the Persecuted Church
Super Sketches for Youth Ministry
Talking the Walk
Teaching the Bible Creatively
Videos That Teach

What Would Jesus Do? Youth Leader's Kit
Wild Truth Bible Lessons
Wild Truth Bible Lessons 2
Wild Truth Bible Lessons—Pictures of God
Worship Services for Youth Groups

Professional Resources

Administration, Publicity, & Fundraising (Ideas Library)
Dynamic Communicators Workshop For Youth Workers
Equipped to Serve: Volunteer Youth Worker Training Course
Great Talk Outlines for Youth Ministry
Help! I'm a Junior High Youth Worker!
Help! I'm a Small-Group Leader!
Help! I'm a Sunday School Teacher!
Help! I'm an Urban Youth Worker!
Help! I'm a Volunteer Youth Worker!
How to Expand Your Youth Ministry
How to Speak to Youth...and Keep Them Awake at the Same Time
Junior High Ministry (Updated & Expanded)
The Ministry of Nurture: A Youth Worker's Guide to Discipling Teenagers
Postmodern Youth Ministry
Purpose-Driven® Youth Ministry
Purpose-Driven® Youth Ministry Training Kit
So That's Why I Keep Doing This! 52 Devotional Stories for Youth Workers
A Youth Ministry Crash Course
Youth Ministry Management Tools
The Youth Worker's Handbook to Family Ministry

Academic Resources

Four Views of Youth Ministry & the Church
Starting Right: Thinking Theologically About Youth Ministry
Youth Ministry That Transforms

Discussion Starters

Discussion & Lesson Starters (Ideas Library)
Discussion & Lesson Starters 2 (Ideas Library)
EdgeTV
Get 'Em Talking
Keep 'Em Talking!
Good Sex: A Whole-Person Approach to Teenage Sexuality & God
High School TalkSheets—Updated!
More High School TalkSheets—Updated!
High School TalkSheets from Psalms and Proverbs Updated!
Junior High-Middle School TalkSheets—Updated!
More Junior High-Middle School TalkSheets—Updated!
Junior High-Middle School TalkSheets from Psalms and Proverbs—Updated!
Real Kids: Short Cuts
Real Kids: The Real Deal—on Friendship, Loneliness, Racism, & Suicide
Real Kids: The Real Deal—on Sexual Choices, Family Matters, & Loss
Real Kids: The Real Deal—on Stressing Out, Addictive Behavior, Great Comebacks, & Violence

Real Kids: Word on the Street
Unfinished Sentences: 450 Tantalizing Statement Starters to Get Teenagers Talking & Thinking
What If...? 450 Thought-Provoking Questions to Get Teenagers Talking, Laughing, and Thinking
Would You Rather...? 465 Provocative Questions to Get Teenagers Talking
Have You Ever...? 450 Intriguing Questions Guaranteed to Get Teenagers Talking

Art Source Clip Art

Stark Raving Clip Art (print)
Youth Group Activities (print)
Clip Art Library Version 2.0 (CD-ROM)

Digital Resources

Clip Art Library Version 2.0 (CD-ROM)
Hot Illustrations CD-ROM
Ideas Library on CD-ROM
Great Talk Outlines for Youth Ministry
Screen Play
Youth Ministry Management Tools

Videos & Video Curricula

Dynamic Communicators Workshop
EdgeTV
Equipped to Serve: Volunteer Youth Worker Training Course
The Heart of Youth Ministry: A Morning with Mike Yaconelli
Live the Life! Student Evangelism Training Kit
Purpose-Driven® Youth Ministry Training Kit
Real Kids: Short Cuts
Real Kids: The Real Deal—on Friendship, Loneliness, Racism, & Suicide
Real Kids: The Real Deal—on Sexual Choices, Family Matters, & Loss
Real Kids: The Real Deal—on Stressing Out, Addictive Behavior, Great Comebacks, & Violence
Real Kids: Word on the Street
Student Underground: An Event Curriculum on the Persecuted Church
Understanding Your Teenager Video Curriculum
Youth Ministry Outside the Lines

Student Resources

Downloading the Bible: A Rough Guide to the New Testament
Downloading the Bible: A Rough Guide to the Old Testament
Grow For It Journal through the Scriptures
So What Am I Gonna Do With My Life?
Spiritual Challenge Journal: The Next Level
Teen Devotional Bible
What (Almost) Nobody Will Tell You about Sex
What Would Jesus Do? Spiritual Challenge Journal
Wild Truth Journal for Junior Highers
Wild Truth Journal—Pictures of God
Wild Truth Journal—Pictures of God 2

Many of the discussion starters in this book appeared in the
Ideas Library, published by Youth Specialties, Inc.

The authors wish to thank all of the creative youth workers
who originally developed these discussion starters
and who contributed them for publication.
Without them, this book would not have been possible.

CONTENTS

PART I ◇ BASIC TRAINING FOR DISCUSSION LEADERS

PART II ◇ DISCUSSION STARTERS

CONTENTS

PART I
BASIC TRAINING for DISCUSSION LEADERS

INTRODUCTION

■ "I used to hate going to Sunday school. Then we got this new teacher—she starts every meeting differently, and we end up in a wild discussion. I learn a lot—I even hate for the meetings to be over."

■ "Get this. Our youth director gets us in this great discussion. Everybody's into it, okay, but he doesn't agree with what we're saying; so he stops the discussion and lectures us on the stuff we were saying. Can you believe it?"

■ "I came home from youth group really upset. We had this discussion on abortion. Everyone was arguing about what was right and wrong. Then our sponsor cut off the discussion with everyone still disagreeing. I was so mad! I went home and told my parents. We spent about two hours talking about the meeting. And then it hit me—that's exactly what our sponsor wanted me to do. I have to admit it worked."

■ "All we do is sit around and talk about whatever. There's no structure, no topic, no nothing. We just sit around every week and talk. It's totally boring."

Few things in youth ministry generate more excitement than experiencing the energy of a great discussion. There's nothing like seeing kids talk with each other after a large, unwieldy youth group gets transformed into small, caring, teenage families.

Everything in this book is geared to help you bring excitement and effectivness to your group's discussion.

First, we've given you the basic steps in planning a discussion that leaves your young people asking for more. Then we've added the best discussion-starting ideas that youth workers around the country have used successfully with their groups.

Feel free to modify, adapt, tear apart, and overhaul these ideas—or use them as sparks for new ideas. Do whatever you need to make these ideas work for you—ideas that can help your young people grow stronger in their faith as they think through sticky life issues, study God's Word, and learn to relate more positively with each other.

Anyone can participate in a discussion but few can effectively lead one. Most people understand the meaning of discussion, but not many can explain what a good discussion is like. Others know exactly what a good discussion is like, they just don't know how to make it happen. *Get 'Em Talking* is for those who want to make bad discussions good, good discussions great, and every discussion significant.

WHY USE DISCUSSION QUESTIONS, ANYWAY?

Misuse of discussion in youth groups has marred its reputation as a credible learning tool. A leader who didn't have time to prepare a lesson or who needs a fill-in until church lets out often abuses the technique of discussion. Having a discussion just because the kids like to talk is another poor reason to structure a meeting around discussing issues. And using discussion questions to set kids up for a lecture on why they shouldn't think that way creates resentful youths. If you've ever slid into any of these errors, you're probably disillusioned and frustrated with using discussion in youth ministry.

But if you've experienced a well-planned and spirited discussion, you know it reaches kids' hearts and minds. A good discussion:

■ develops youth group togetherness.
■ encourages young people to tell each other about their thoughts, feelings, and opinions. A personal question requires a personal answer.
■ enables young people to use information for personal growth.
■ allows young people to think and respond with their heads and their hearts.
■ facilitates learning without adult domination.
■ helps a leader evaluate a teenager's knowledge about and understanding of a specific topic.

Discussing in Small Groups Builds Community

If discussion questions are the foundation of a successful youth group learning experience, then discussion groups are the walls and roof. And walls and roofs have never been more important to a youth group. Today the give and take of conversation has been replaced by small talk and television. Kids are more likely to experience close fellowship with Nintendo games. Discussion, however, is a community activity. Young people hear and respond to each other while trading ideas together. Individuals subject their ideas to the scrutiny of the entire group, creating for the group an identity separate from each individual.

Discussing Ideas Matures Relational Skills

It doesn't take long to discover that merely asking young people to sit in a circle on the floor and carry on a meaningful discussion ends in disappointment and wasted time. While teenagers spend a great deal of time talking, most have yet to develop the skills and attitudes necessary for making the most of group discussion.

A discussion group can be an ideal environment for young people to learn the skills it takes to talk with, listen to, and learn from each other and from adults. In a constructive discussion group participants learn to:

■ take turns speaking, listening, and learning.
■ check their understanding of reality.
■ value each person's opinions and experiences.
■ experiment with new thoughts, opinions, and ideas in a living laboratory.

Think about it. Where can young people practice relational skills when most church and school settings restrict learning to students listening to adults? Discussions equalize the interaction, requiring participants to speak and listen.

Discussing Issues Stimulates Turning Ideas into Action

Animated discussion overflows into other contexts—home, school, and church. If the kids enjoy the discussion, then they bring up the ideas to their parents and friends and continue talking about what they're learning. After trying ideas out by first talking about them, young people are more likely to discover changes creeping into their lifestyles and bottom-line thinking on an issue.

Discussing Enhances Learning

You've probably heard this before, and it's true: We remember less than 10% of what we hear. But we remember over 80% of what we experience. Discussion groups move teenagers from impassive listening to deeper involvement with each other as they share their thoughts about the topic that's being discussed.

Edgar Dale, professor of education at The Ohio State University, places discussion right next to direct, personal experience in percent of retained information. The more the method of presenting information involves the student in the process, the greater the amount of information he remembers.

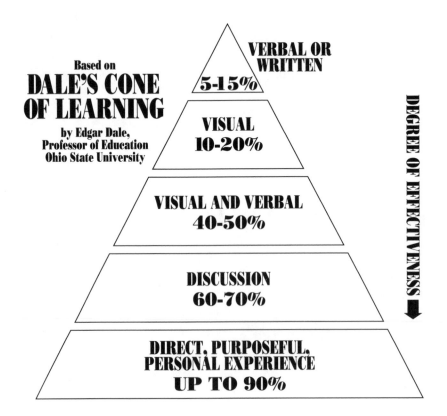

Based on
DALE'S CONE OF LEARNING
by Edgar Dale,
Professor of Education
Ohio State University

VERBAL OR WRITTEN
5-15%

VISUAL
10-20%

VISUAL AND VERBAL
40-50%

DISCUSSION
60-70%

DIRECT, PURPOSEFUL, PERSONAL EXPERIENCE
UP TO 90%

DEGREE OF EFFECTIVENESS

If you've been in many discussion groups, you know that no two discussions are the same. One discussion might generate so much energy that the electricty you feel could light up an entire city. Yet, the same group on another day might need jumper cables and a heavy duty battery to get the discussion started.

What makes for a discussion group that crackles and pops with energy?

WHAT ARE THE INGREDIENTS OF A GREAT DISCUSSION?

Create a Great Discussion by Choosing a Relevant, Specific Topic

"Being filled with the Spirit" may be a topic kids need to talk about, but if it sounds dull, your discussion won't get off the ground. To connect that session to kids' lives, announce a discussion titled "Holy Ghostbusters! Is the Holy Spirit Weird?" Spark interest in attending a Bible study on sexuality with the question, "Did Jesus Have Hormones?" or "Sex: Is Everyone Just Saying Yes?"

The more personal the content, the stronger the discussion. Talking about world hunger after reading aloud a pamphlet won't have the impact of debriefing after working for a day in a soup kitchen downtown.

Even if you have an relevant topic, the discussion can flounder if the topic is too broad. If you're discussing self-esteem, for instance, focus the dialogue by asking, "How can you feel worthwhile when your parents never

Five Ground Rules for a Great Discussion

1. *What is said in this room stays in this room.* Confidentiality is vital to a healthy discussion. The only time it should be broken is when a group member reveals plans to harm himself or another person.
2. *No put-downs.* Sarcasm and unkind remarks have no place in a discussion. If someone disagrees with another's comment, she should raise her hand and express her opinion of the comment, but not of the person who made it. It is permissible to attack ideas, but not each other.
3. *There is no such thing as a dumb question.* Asking questions is the best way to learn.
4. *No one is forced to talk.* Anyone can remain silent about any question.
5. *Only one person talks at a time.* Each person's opinion is worthwhile and deserves to be heard. Listening is an expression of respect. ◇

think you do anything right?" or "Who cares if God loves you if everyone else thinks you're a jerk?" Or if you want to talk about death, choose a specific aspect of death—death of a parent, what happens after death, funerals, suicide, helping people who have had a death in their family, fear of death, coping with death. The more specific the topic, the livelier the discussion.

Create a Great Discussion with Intriguing Publicity

Publicity for a discussion should create interest and generate enthusiasm. Are you exploring parent/child relationships? Tell the kids that tonight you'll be discussing the question, "Are parents human?" Or give them a discussion starter in booklet form called "How To Survive Your Parents." Send the book of Hosea to the top of your students' reading list by advance publicity using this question, "Would God Want You To Marry a Prostitute?"

Overcome resistance to tackling a discouraging or frightening issue like depression or suicide by a heading like "Suicide: Has anyone not considered it?" or "Depression: a Gift from God." Begin to shape understanding for a much talked about word like *grace* by asking "Does God Forgive You When You Sin on Purpose?" or "God Loves Us...But Does He Like Us?" A young person who anticipates a discussion comes prepared with specific thoughts on the subject that launch the discussion.

Create a Great Discussion with Open-Ended Questions

There are really only two kinds of discussion questions—good discussion questions and bad discussion questions. Good discussion questions invite people to talk, motivate them to contribute, encourage participation, stimulate new questions, and affirm the significance of each person's opinion. Bad discussion questions discourage participation, affirm that only the leader's opinion matters, threaten timid contributors, and motivate the group to keep quiet.

Good questions focus on a person's opinion (What would you tell a friend who asked you if she should get an abortion?) or his experience (Has anyone ever known someone who tried to commit suicide?) or personal values (If someone offered you a beer at a party, what would you do?) or a person's faith (When you are depressed, does your faith in God make any difference?). Bad questions assume there is one right answer or don't require any answer at all.

The following are examples of bad questions—questions that stifle discussion:

■ **Loaded questions.** Who should our example be, the Apostle Paul or Charles Manson? Do kids who drink at parties have a lot of fun, or do they just think they are having fun? Some people who call themselves Christians say they believe that abortion is okay, but what does the Bible say?

■ **Fill-in-the-blank questions.** John 3:16 says, God so loved the what? And that whosoever what shall not what? How do we know that God so loved the world?

■ **Rhetorical questions.** Since God made our bodies, don't you think he would have a good reason to say that getting drunk is wrong? God knows what's best for us, so don't you think you should listen when he says that sexual contact before marriage is destructive? Our bodies are the temple of God, so what should you do about smoking?

■ **Intimidating questions.** If you really loved God, what should you do? Obviously, God is telling us to what? This is a famous parable, John, what do you think it means? Jesus is making three powerful statements here, what are they? Do you think God is pleased with what we've just talked about?

Good questions create an open, accepting atmosphere that lets every participant in the discussion know that every contribution is appreciated. Bad questions create a closed, threatening atmosphere that lets every participant in the discussion know that only acceptable contributions are appreciated.

Using Questions to Keep a Discussion Going

The ideas on pages 42-160 give you dozens of creative ways to start your young people talking—but it's up to you to keep discussion going by asking clarifying questions, by helping the group members resolve conflicts, by probing issues more deeply, and by involving everyone in the discussion and relationship-building process.

Use these questions to *clarify* what someone just said:
* "Can you give me an example or two about..."
* "What do you mean by...?"
* "Why do you believe that?"
* "What is the basis for your conclusion/feelings?"
* "Would you explain what you just said for us?"

To resolve conflict, make statements like the following:
* "Have we really heard what you're trying to say, Mark?"

* "I had no idea everyone felt so strongly about this. Let's take a two-minute break, and when we come back together, let's answer this question..."
* "It looks like we need to do some more research on this idea. Let's go on to the next question and come back to this next week."

If you want to probe or go more deeply into an answer, ask these kinds of questions:
* "What else are you feeling?"
* "Could you tell me more about...?"
* "Could you explain what you mean by...?"
* "What else can you tell us about...?"

To redirect the discussion to someone else, try these ideas:
* "Jane, what do you think about what Alex just said?"
* "Let's hear what Bob thinks."
* "John, I'm glad you've got so much to say on this topic. I wonder if anyone else has something to add."

If after trying to keep a discussion going you still have some in your group who resist participating, they probably had a bad experience talking in a group. The only way to overcome the damage done by bad experiences is to start having good experiences. First, ask the kids to honestly describe the bad experiences and explain why those discussions made them so uncomfortable. Second, demonstrate that you learned from their frankness by changing your approaches to leading discussions. To give your discussions a running start, invite an experienced and successful discussion leader to kick off your series. ◇

Create a Great Discussion by Grooming Listeners

The pitfall in group discussion isn't necessarily teenagers who won't talk, but teenagers who don't listen. Listening is the art of both hearing and feeling what someone else is saying. A listener genuinely focuses on the speaker's communication with empathy and respect. A listener sets aside her opinions and judgments so she can experience what the speaker is sharing. Empathy—putting oneself in someone else's shoes—instead of sympathy—"I feel that way, too"—characterizes a listener.

A listener restates in his own words what he believes the speaker has said. Hearing a paraphrase lets the speaker know that the listener identifies with his feelings and helps the speaker sort out his own feelings. Paraphrasing keeps advice giving to a minimum without smothering discussion. A listener resists the urge to judge what the speaker is saying, but allows her to paint the entire picture with both words and feelings.

A listener keeps confidences. It's unrealistic to expect that a youth group has no information leaks. So encourage kids to be honest but not irresponsible about what they share in the group setting. Public sharing has restraints that private sharing does not. If someone needs to share private questions or feelings, invite him to talk to you or another adult later.

A listener is kind. If kids are fearful of criticism, ridicule, or put-downs, they won't talk. Although youth leaders don't allow those kinds of remarks among the youths, leaders and kids alike sometimes incorporate a certain level of repartee based on ridicule, criticism, and put-downs. Some groups relate among themselves only in sarcastic remarks—their smart-aleck personality is part of the bond that holds the group together. Yet that kind of bond halts the growth of loving community. As leader you can help the kids face the problem and determine steps for changing the way they speak to each other.

Create a Great Discussion by Grooming a Leader

We all have visions of the type of person who makes a great discussion leader. For some, it's the person who has limitless energy, effortless charisma, a complete knowledge of group dynamics, and earned degrees in Bible history, theology,

What's Your LQ? (Leadership Quotient)

Rate yourself on the following qualities of great discussion leaders. Rate yourself on how you exhibit these qualities.

1. I like the kids in my group and I trust them to make thoughtful responses to discussion questions.
Me 10 9 8 7 6 5 4 3 2 1 *Not Me*

2. My actions and attitudes encourage the young people in my group to work toward the group's goals.
Me 10 9 8 7 6 5 4 3 2 1 *Not Me*

3. I resist the temptation to do everything myself—I'd rather let young people find their own answers.
Me 10 9 8 7 6 5 4 3 2 1 *Not Me*

4. I allow the people in my group to try different roles and behaviors.
Me 10 9 8 7 6 5 4 3 2 1 *Not Me*

5. I let my group know it's okay to learn by trial and error.
Me 10 9 8 7 6 5 4 3 2 1 *Not Me*

6. I'm not afraid to say, "I don't know."
Me 10 9 8 7 6 5 4 3 2 1 *Not Me*

7. I help people in my group clarify their thoughts and feelings by paraphrasing what I think I hear them saying.
Me 10 9 8 7 6 5 4 3 2 1 *Not Me*

8. I discourage negative, punitive, exaggerated, critical, and rude remarks.
Me 10 9 8 7 6 5 4 3 2 1 *Not Me*

9. I allow time for thinking when I ask a question that requires reflection.
Me 10 9 8 7 6 5 4 3 2 1 *Not Me*

10. I encourage discussion by commenting on positive remarks and asking questions that ask for an additional response.
Me 10 9 8 7 6 5 4 3 2 1 *Not Me*

11. I allow periods of silence without jumping in with additional comments or questions.
Me 10 9 8 7 6 5 4 3 2 1 *Not Me*

12. I keep myself from interrupting a good discussion with my own thoughts and feelings.
Me 10 9 8 7 6 5 4 3 2 1 *Not Me*

13. I use the natural breaking points in a discussion as opportunities to review the group's progress and growth.
Me 10 9 8 7 6 5 4 3 2 1 *Not Me*

14. I periodically evaluate the progress individual group members are making toward personal and spiritual growth.
Me 10 9 8 7 6 5 4 3 2 1 *Not Me*

15. I celebrate positive experiences with the group.
Me 10 9 8 7 6 5 4 3 2 1 *Not Me*

16. I help the group pace its discussion so that everyone who wants to can add something to the discussion.
Me 10 9 8 7 6 5 4 3 2 1 *Not Me*

17. I work to identify and remove barriers to group and individual growth.
Me 10 9 8 7 6 5 4 3 2 1 *Not Me*

18. I give time limits on discussion topics, if necessary, so the group can cover a number of different issues.
Me 10 9 8 7 6 5 4 3 2 1 *Not Me*

19. I have chosen a location that encourages discussion with a casual seating arrangement, appropriate lighting, minimal distractions, and comfortable room temperature.
Me 10 9 8 7 6 5 4 3 2 1 *Not Me*

20. I come to the discussion prepared with whatever it takes to encourage discovery and discussion: paper, pencils, Bibles, handouts, overhead, chalkboard, props, etc.
Me 10 9 8 7 6 5 4 3 2 1 *Not Me*

What are your strongest areas?

What areas can use some improvement?

What specific steps can you take to strengthen the weak areas? ◇

adolescent development, and psychoanalysis. For others, a perfect leader is the person whose presence alone transforms rowdy kids into quiet, reverent, teenage theologians.

What's your vision of the perfect leader? Take a moment now to picture that person in your mind.

Now forget it. Youth groups don't need super slick discussion leaders. What they do need is someone who is open, can facilitate with neutrality, likes kids, knows how to make transitions, and keeps confidences.

Open. A good discussion leader hears out all points of view, even when a point of view is wrong in his opinion. Although the leader may not agree with what she hears, her openness creates trust in the kids—a feeling that the thoughts they struggle with don't make them unacceptable.

Neutral. A good discussion leader does not use his opinion to manipulate the discussion or overpower someone he disagrees with. She keeps her emotional distance and doesn't make comments that give away her beliefs. A neutral leader gives his opinion when asked, but concentrates on facilitating communication among the kids.

Likes kids. Because kids get silly, wander off the subject, don't follow the discussion, and generally act like kids, a good discussion leader has to like kids. Leading kids in a discussion requires the patience of one who knows why kids act the way they do and accepts them at that point in their maturing process.

Makes transitions. A good discussion leader recognizes a floundering discussion and either steers a new course with alternate questions (see Using Questions To Keep a Discussion Going, p. 20) or ends the discussion. Sometimes a pause means that the kids are thinking about what they want to say or that the entire group needs silence to process information and feelings. Don't be intimidated by constructive silence. Sometimes, however, a lull in talking means that the discussion is over. A discerning leader will learn to recognize the meaning of a silence and make appropriate transitions from discussion to another element of the program.

Keeps confidences. Thoughts the kids share in youth group must be kept confidential by both kids and leaders. If youths feel that what they say will be repeated to their parents or other adults, they will clam up. A zealous sponsor, after hearing one of the teens talk about drinking at a party, being sexually experienced, or lying to her parents, may feel it is his duty to inform that teen's parents or to tell other church members. Remind him that information shared during discussion is confidential. Leaders who do not honor the trust the teens show when they share intimate thoughts should be removed from leadership. Don't penalize kids for being honest.

DISCUSSION STYLES

Topical Discussions

The purpose of a topical discussion is to discover

- what the group knows about the topic,

- why this topic is significant to adolescents,

- what issues are connected with the topic,

- how your kids feel about the topic,

- what problems the topic poses for them,

- how they can deal with the problems.

Creative Discussion Materials

Junior High Talksheets, Zondervan/Youth Specialties
High School Talksheets, Zondervan/Youth Specialties
Tension Getters, Zondervan/Youth Specialties
Tension Getters II, Zondervan/Youth Specialties
Amazing Tension Getters, Zondervan/Youth Specialties
Good Clean Fun, Zondervan/Youth Specialties
Good Clean Fun II, Zondervan/Youth Specialties
To Do Or Not To Do, Drug and Alcohol Talk Box, Youth Specialties
Yes, No or Maybe So, Sexuality Talk Box, Youth Specialties
Roll-A-Role, Youth Specialties
Rock n' Roll Teacher, Youth Specialties
Good News Q's, Youth Specialties ◇

Discussions That Teach

Teaching discussions follow a lecture, a movie, a Bible study, a sermon, or the reading of a book. This kind of discussion usually asks questions like

■ What did you learn?

■ What did you not understand?

■ What are the implications of this study?

The difference between discussing a topic and discussing a film or lecture is how much the participants know about the subject.

Discussing Feelings

Suppose, for example, that one of the adult sponsors is dying of cancer, and the youth group is upset and confused. Kids can process their experiences by sharing with each other their feelings and exploring what to do with these feelings. If a young person says he is feeling angry that a person so young is dying of cancer,

the leader can prompt discussion by asking questions like, "Why are you feeling so angry?" "Does anyone else feel that way?" "Is anger in this situation justified?" "Those of you that don't feel angry, why don't you feel anger?" "What do you feel?"

Discussing Opinions

To find out what your group believes about a topic or subject, discuss the kids' opinions about it in an atmosphere

where they feel comfortable expressing what they think as well as what they don't know. Discussing their opinions better equips you to teach the kind of information they need to handle that topic.

When the young people in your group are 14 and under, the dynamics of discussion change. The questions must be open-ended—not questions that threaten them with having to give the right answer. The leader must be direct instead of subtly staying in the background. And the discussion must be short. Sharing opinions is one of the best ways to help younger kids talk freely. Even then, however, they talk to the leader more than to each other.

How to Brainstorm

Use this simple technique any time you need a bunch of ideas on any one topic:

1. Make sure everyone understands exactly what the topic or problem is. Write it down so everyone can see it.

2. Allow a few minutes for individuals to write down as many ideas on their own as they can—the crazier the ideas, the better.

3. Ask each person to give you one idea from his list that he really likes. Write each idea on a chalkboard, overhead, or flip chart.

4. Using the list you just made as a springboard, ask the group to toss out as many ideas as they can about each idea on the board. At this point, don't let kids judge an idea as good or bad.

5. If you need more ideas, repeat the process for each person's second best idea.

6. Once you have exhausted the group's new ideas, ask everyone to choose the ideas from the list that best fit the topic or problem you outlined in step 1.

7. Refine the ideas you just listed. ◇

Discussions That Strengthen Relationships

The subject of a discussion is often secondary to student interaction during the discussion. Since one of the goals of a discussion is to build relationships between the young people, you can double its community-building potential by talking about "Who I Am." Lyman Coleman's *Serendipity* materials offer questions that make it easy for kids to reveal thoughts and feelings about themselves in an atmosphere of trust, affirmation, empathy, and community.

Serendipity Questions

1. The place I retreat to when I need to "get myself together" is (circle one):
a. the park
b. a lake
c. fishing spot
d. the bathtub
e. TV
f. the woods
g. a quiet chapel
h. a ball game
i. the movies
j. the beach
k. the mountains
l. an easy chair
m. my room
n. out of the house
o. anywhere

2. My philosophy of life might be summarized by the phrase (circle first and last choice):
a. if it feels good, do it
b. what the heck
c. grab all the gusto you can
d. love and be happy
e. do unto others as you want them to do unto you
f. look out for number one
g. roll with the punches
h. I don't want to grow up
i. if you want something bad enough, you'll get it

3. The hardest decisions for me are usually when (rank top three):
___money is involved
___friendship is involved
___my reputation is on the line
___my popularity is at stake
___my moral values are involved

4. The biggest fear I have to deal with in standing up for what I believe is (circle one):
a. being laughed at
b. standing alone
c. getting someone else in trouble
d. being wrong
e. losing my friends
f. _____

Learn more about Lyman Coleman's *Serendipity* materials by writing to Serendipity House, Box 1012, Littleton, CO 80160. ◇

Discussions About Scripture

Skillfully written questions can guide a group to analyze, interpret, and explain what the Scripture says and then to steer them to evaluate their lives in light of that Scripture. Here are questions about two Scripture passages that are not loaded or intimidating but invite participation. (You can find great Scripture questions in *Good News Q's*, published by Youth Specialties.)

Questions about Matthew 4:1-11

■ What is temptation?

■ When was the last time you were tempted?

■ Jesus was in a weakened condition when He was tempted. When are you in a weakened condition?

■ Jesus quoted Scripture to battle his temptation. What works for you when you are being tempted?

Questions about John 1:1-18

■ How is Jesus life and light?

■ Have you ever experienced the life and light of Jesus?

■ Have you ever experienced the darkness of being without Christ?

■ Why do people sometimes reject the light and head for the darkness?

■ Why can darkness be so appealing?

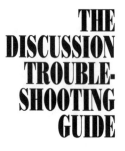

THE DISCUSSION TROUBLE-SHOOTING GUIDE

■ Someone starts talking about an idea that has nothing to do with the topic you're discussing. Yet, the entire group gets wrapped up in talking about the new, unrelated topic.

■ One person either starts attacking someone else or becomes the target of the rest of the group.

■ The discussion turns into an advice-giving session.

■ The discussion topic triggers strong feelings in several young people, and the meeting turns into a gripe session.

Struggling through any of these frustrating attempts at discussion turns leaders off to that kind of meeting. But the helpful solutions that follow can turn a group that is sour on discussion into lively, focused communicators.

Problem #1: What do I do when the discussion gets sidetracked?

A discussion can get sidetracked because it was poorly planned or poorly led or because the kind of thing the kids are discussing is suited to freewheeling and even boisterous responses.

The first rule in any discussion is to decide what you want that discussion to do. If your goal is to make kids aware of their feelings about a certain topic or to find out where your kids are at, for instance, getting as many statements as you can from as many kids as possible may give the meeting a hectic feel. If your purpose is to help kids understand what their options are in a particular situation, then you're looking for specific suggestions and comments directed at that one issue. This kind of discussion may stay more on track.

Some people do not have the personality or the skills to lead a discussion. They may dislike confronting people or else confront them with the grace of a drill sergeant. These workers are equipped to become resourceful leaders in something other than leading discussions with adolescents.

Return a sidetracked discussion to its focus by redirecting the conversation. Say something like, "This has really been interesting, but I think we're getting a little bit off the subject. Let's go back to the question I asked earlier." Then restate the original question.

Keep the discussion on track by taking tension breaks. When you sense emotions building toward a free-for-all, say something like, "Wow, I had no idea everyone felt so strongly about this. Let's take a break for a couple of minutes, and when we come back I would like to ask..." Or help the kids leave the subject entirely by saying, "Hey, this is a hot subject. I'll tell you what, let's go on to another question, and next week we'll spend the whole meeting talking about this."

Sometimes a discussion is so far gone that the best way to restore order is to end the discussion. Calmly ask everyone to stop talking and listen to you summarize the comments that did relate to the topic. Then close the meeting or move on to another activity.

Problem #2: What do I do when we're discussing controversial subjects?

An exciting, wonderful thing can happen when you take a group of young people and stir them up so they:

■ contribute on a personal level;

■ express warm and positive feelings as well as anger, frustration, and discouragement;

■ encourage and build each other up;

■ try to understand and appreciate each other;

■ are vulnerable with each other, because they know they're accepted for who they are;

■ take time to listen and to understand each other; and

■ make other group members feel welcome and appreciated.

That wonderful thing is conflict. Though conflict can be frustrating, it is the fertilizer that helps people in the group grow personally and spiritually.

Intervening in youth group conflict in loving and caring ways is the key to turning conflict into positive growth experiences.

Following these basic guidelines will make talking about controversial topics much easier:

■ **Know your kids well.** Some young people are not ready to confront certain problems. Discussing death when one of your kid's parents is dying may be untimely—then again, it may be the perfect time. To make that decision you have to know your kids well.

If the group appears reluctant or fearful of a topic, respect their hesitancy and back off. Analyze for yourself why the group has a difficult time with a subject. Are they too young? Does their ethnic background have anything to do with it? Are you expecting them to be comfortable with something it took you twenty years to be comfortable with? Are you more blunt and straightforward than the kids in your group because of your background or upbringing? Model for them the discretion you hope they'll learn to use when they talk together.

■ **Don't dump on kids.** Many issues of our faith are difficult for even adults to sort out. Balance these issues with discussions of non-controversial foundations of faith. As young people mature, they not only learn more, but they learn to handle more ambiguity.

■ **Don't try to shock kids for effect.** If you play the devil's advocate, make sure your arguments are sensible. Don't always shoot holes through your kids' arguments just to create conflict. Shocking kids with extreme positions often causes kids to treat the discussion more like a skit, and it degenerates into silliness.

■ **Give people time.** Let the young people go home thinking. Not every issue can be resolved in 60 minutes, as TV leads us to believe. When young people carry an unresolved issue, they usually end up talking with parents or friends about it.

That dialogue can be more productive than a neat resolution in youth group.

■ **Don't be afraid of controversy or failure.** When you discuss a controversial issue, leave it unresolved, or disturb comfortable beliefs, you will be criticized by both young people and parents. Sometimes the criticism is justified because youth leaders do make mistakes. Sometimes your mistake causes a young person to drop out of the group. That is a risk of growth. Admit your mistakes, learn from your failures, but don't back off simply because you have pushed people—including yourself—into new areas of maturity.

Problem #3: Why do my discussions always fall flat?

Healthy discussion groups have that warm, relaxed, accepting, non-threatening feel. This positive youth group environment invites young people to feel open, honest, and real. Creating that feeling when the kids first walk in is the first step to resurrecting enthusiasm for discussing. The appearance of the room and the make-up of the group cooperate to produce the right feel for an energized discussion.

■ **Size.** Generally, the larger the group, the more impersonal it becomes. A shy or discouraged person can easily hide out in a large group. People who lead a large-group discussion tend to be firmer and more directive, resulting in less interaction and discussion among group members. Divide into groups of four to revitalize large group discussion with small group input.

In a small group, however, where kids may know each other well, they can grow tired of each other. Taking a break from discussions for a special speaker, a film, a video, or a music group lets discussion sparkle when you come back to it.

In either small or large groups, beginning a discussion with ice-breaking games or skits can free kids to enter whole-heartedly into talking with each other. Ask non-threatening questions (What is your favorite movie and why?) that help the group get to know each other before tackling more threatening questions (What's the biggest problem you face with your parents?).

■ **Frequency of meetings.** The more often a group meets, the closer the members become to each other. For instance, monthly meetings usually limit a discussion's depth—both the depth of the information you discuss and the deepening of relationships—because the young people don't know each other very well. On the other hand, groups that meet weekly tend to become more open, with group members willing to tackle difficult issues and topics.

■ **Setting.** The best place to hold a discussion is a well lit, cheery room, just large enough for the group and free from outside noise and distractions. The closer you can get to a homey, family-room feeling, the better. Cavernous fellowship halls, gyms, or sanctuaries kill discussion. It's better to use a room that's too small than to use one that's

---

Fifteen ways to get kids talking

1. Start with non-threatening questions.

2. Begin with questions that ask for opinions.

3. Instead of starting with a question, begin with a role-play, case study, or tension getter that provokes a response.

4. Give your opinion about the question and ask the kids to respond to it.

5. Ask the kids to anonymously write down their responses to a question or topic. Collect their papers to read aloud; then let the kids respond to what they wrote.

6. If the group is large, divide into smaller groups that discuss the issue then report their conclusions to the larger group.

7. If the group combines 12-year-olds with 16-year-olds, for example, divide into groups of similar ages.

8. Ask the kids why they are not talking; discuss their responses to that question.

9. Make the dialogue seem more like a game with discussion starters like TalkSheets, Talk Boxes, or Role-A-Role.

10. Play Round-Robin with discussion leaders—students take turns asking the questions that keep discussion moving, as well as responding to other kids' comments.

11. Brainstorm all the possible responses to the question.

12. Ask all adults to leave the room while the kids discuss the questions on their own. When the time limit is up, the adults return to hear the kids' report on what they discussed.

13. Give the kids a survey; discuss the results.

14. End the meeting formally, then informally bring up some of the issues of the discussion.

15. Forget the discussion this time and try it some other time. ◇

---

too large.

■ **Seating arrangement.** Since people who can see each other are most likely to carry on a discussion, the best seating arrangement is a circle. Everyone has a chance to look at whoever's talking. Circles have their own dead spots, however. The person who sits across from the leader has the most direct eye contact and is most likely to talk. Those people who sit on the leader's immediate right or left are least likely to talk because it's difficult for them to make direct eye contact with the leader.

■ **Ratio of leaders to kids.** Too many adult sponsors intimidate kids, especially if they aggressively participate in the discussion. There is no magic ratio of adults to kids. Let your group's comfort level determine the number of advisors attending. The presence of parents usually inhibits free interaction—no matter how cool the parents are. The more neutral the adults in a discussion, the more open the kids will be.

■ **Age range.** If the kids in your group are separated in age by more than four years, a discussion will probably flounder. Divide into groups of similar ages before starting, or ask another leader to take the younger kids to a separate room for the part of the meeting that includes discussion.

Problem #4: What do I do about kids who make it practically impossible to have a good discussion?

If you want your discussion group to be a living laboratory of personal discovery and spiritual growth, expect some problems. When young people feel more comfortable with each other and their defenses start to drop, then personality and behavioral quirks emerge. As growth and transformation take place, your young people will be exposed to each other's unloving attitudes and behaviors. But, as high school football players put it, "No pain, no gain!" Discussion groups are a little like that. Whatever pain you experience will be offset by your group members' personal and spiritual growth. It's all worth the effort.

As your young people experiment with vulnerability, you're likely to run across some stereotypical personalities. Here are a few of the more predictable ones, plus ideas for handling them in a discussion-group setting.

The Expert

The self-acclaimed expert always knows just what the problem is and just what to do to fix it. He acts like he has the correct point of view. The best strategy with a person like this is to convincingly bring up another point of view or play the devil's advocate. Or you can say, "That makes sense, Debra, but what would you say to those who would argue...?" If the group is intimidated by The Expert, then it is effective if you as a leader disagree with her. It gives the others courage to state their disagreements.

The Talker

Talk, talk, talk. The Talker usually doesn't know if what he's saying is interesting or helpful—he's too busy talking. This person is often the first to respond to a question. And the answer is generally a stream-of-consciousness monologue that never seems to end. Talkers find it hard to accept the

discipline of being part of a group. Teach The Talker to be sensitive to the other group members by instructing the group in general about communication skills. And when The Talker starts rambling, wait for him to take a breath, then interrupt by saying something like, "Thanks, Clyde, for your thoughts. Cathy, what do you think about...?"

The Silent One

At first glance you might think this person who never contributes to the discussion isn't paying attention. But if a quick reading of her body language tells you that she is listening intently, don't worry about her. There are many people who are not verbal but still follow a discussion with interest. Periodically test The Silent One's readiness to begin to contribute to the discussion by asking a direct question: "Alice, what do you think about...?" Phrasing a question in "feeling" terms might also encourage an answer.

If, on the other hand, The Silent One won't speak out of defiance or because he doesn't like you, then confront him privately. Some kids want the attention of a public confrontation, that's why they're not talking. The best strategy with those who are deliberately silent is to ignore their silence during the meeting and then confront them privately later.

The Negative One

Nothing pleases this person more than finding fault with everything. The Negative One often expects—and receives—the worst from life. And that attitude is contagious; it can infect the whole group if you let it. Confront this person—realizing that to him the confrontation is just another negative experience. The Negative One needs direct help framed in love and understanding to overcome his negative ways.

The Peacemaker

Having grown up in an environment governed by peace at any price, The Peacemaker thinks disagreement means failure. When you notice someone who is compliant, ask yourself if this person really shares the point of view of the speaker or if she is afraid of conflict. Remind the entire group that it's okay to disagree, and help the group develop simple rules for disagreeing. This might help The Peacemaker to feel better about the conflict that occurs naturally in a healthy group. When The Peacemaker intervenes during disagreement to stop the conflict short of resolution and discovery, privately ask him to let those in conflict work things out for themselves.

The Bomb

Warning: This person has a burning fuse and can explode at any time. The Bomb often feels irritated and rarely says what's on his mind. When The Bomb finally explodes in the discussion group, give him the opportunity to express his feelings honestly, without hurting others, of course. Don't panic at the impact that the explosion might have on the group members. Once the anger subsides, reinforce your willingness to hear him out anytime. Encourage this person to share his feelings at regular intervals, which helps keep his anger from building.

The Domineering One

This person loves to be the boss, to dominate everything that happens in the group. The Domineering One doesn't like to be left out. She always has something earth-shattering to share. Her dominating nature often stems from either a false sense of superiority or an energetic enthusiasm to have things be done the right way—her way. Whatever the motivation, The Domineering One usually squelches the group's caring openness and creative discovery. His insensitivity usually stops the give-and-take of a healthy discussion.

The Domineering One often responds to others with resentment and impatience when things do not go her way. While affirming his skills and ability, you can gently (and privately) explain to this person that his actions can be interpreted as rudeness and lack of caring. Suggest that as part of developing good communication skills she refrain from saying anything in the next discussion, devoting her energy to listening instead. Meet again after that discussion and evaluate what happened in the meeting. Keep monitoring the situation until The Domineering One learns some sensitivity and self-control.

Three-Step Plan for Making the Best of Difficult Situations

Each of these personalities can benefit from being part of a discussion group. As soon as you recognize that one of them is hindering the discussion, with gentle confrontation put the discussion back on track. Here's a three-step plan to make the best of difficult situations.

■ **Step One:** Model a caring response.

■ **Step Two:** Come alongside one who is under attack.

■ **Step Three:** Confront the group with their inappropriate communication.

Suppose, for example, that during a discussion, David, one of the group members, says that he feels worn out because his parents are pressuring him to do well academically, practice the piano, and perform well on the soccer team.

Claire responds, "Yeah, that's no good. That much pressure will really make you crazy," implying that David needs to cut out some of his activities. Paul complicates the discussion when he says, "Oh, don't be such a wimp. It can't be that bad."

Scott, sensing that the others haven't understood what David is trying to say, adds his advice, "What you really need, Dave, is to get away from all the hassles for a while. You'll be okay. All you need is a little rest."

"Are you kidding?" David replies. "The last thing I need to do is to get further behind. Then my parents will really get mad at me!"

Remembering that it's natural for group members to want to give advice, you model a caring response (step one): "David, it sounds as though you're tired of having to do well at everything you do. Is that right?"

With a smile on his face, David replies, "Yeah, that's how I feel all right."

As though he hadn't heard the last interaction, Wayne jumps in with, "Well, you need to quit the soccer team."

"C'mon, Dave," adds Tina. "You're old enough to do what you want to do. Tell your parents to take it easy on you or you'll quit everything."

Now's the time to support David (step two). You respond, "David, it seems to me that as a group we haven't really heard what you're trying to say. Can you tell us again what you're really feeling?"

David says that he was thinking that the group would understand what he's feeling and would... But before he can complete the sentence, Chris interrupts: "Dave, it's your life. Tell everyone else to shut up!"

With Chris' response you sense that it's time to confront the group (step three) concerning their advice-giving and criticism. You say, "David has been trying to give us his honest feelings and thoughts. But all we've done is either criticize him or give him advice. I think it's time for us to focus on *hearing and feeling* what David is really saying."

Then allow David to continue. Once David has finished talking, ask everyone what they heard David say and how they think he feels. Ask David to verify those messages.

Here's a quick reference guide to direct you to parts of this book to help you handle specific problems.

1. The topic is not interesting. See "Create a Great Discussion by Choosing a Relevant, Specific Topic," p. 17.

2. The questions are too threatening. See "Create a Great Discussion with Open-Ended Questions," p. 19.

3. The kids don't know anything about the subject. See "Discussion Styles," p. 24.

4. The topic is too broad and the group doesn't know where to start. See "Create a Great Discussion by Choosing a Relevant, Specific Topic," p. 17.

5. There are only three or four kids in the group and they are too shy to talk. See "Why do my discussions always fall flat?—Size," p. 31.

6. The kids are too young. See "Why do my discussions always fall flat?—Age range," p. 33 and "Discussing Opinions," p. 25.

IF THEY WON'T TALK: A TROUBLE-SHOOTER'S INDEX

7. There are too many adult sponsors—the kids feel like a minority. See "Why do my discussions always fall flat?—Ratio of leaders to kids," p. 33.

8. The topic is too sensitive. See "What do I do when we're discussing controversial subjects?" p. 30.

9. The kids do not trust the leaders. See "Create a Great Discussion by Grooming a Leader—Keeps confidences," p. 23.

10. The kids do not trust each other. See "Create a Great Discussion by Grooming Listeners," p. 21.

11. There are too many parents in the group. See "Why do my discussions always fall flat?—Ratio of leaders to kids," p. 33.

12. During previous discussions they have had bad experiences. See "Using Questions to Keep a Discussion Going," p. 20.

13. They are tired of doing discussions every week. (The solution is simple—quit having discussions every week. Variety is important to any group of people, but especially to young people.)

14. They can sense that you are not prepared. See "Why Use Discussion Questions, Anyway?" p. 14.

15. There is too wide of an age spread. See "Why do my discussions always fall flat?—Age range," p. 33.

16. Kids are afraid they will be criticized, ridiculed or put down. See "Create a Great Discussion by Grooming Listeners," p. 21.

17. Sometimes groups are in a bad mood. (Cancel the discussion, lighten up, read aloud a good short story, watch a film, take a walk together.)

18. One person always dominates the discussion. See "The Domineering One," p. 35.

RESOURCES

Clemmons, W., and Harvey Herster. *Growth Through Groups*, Nashville: Broadman Press, 1974.

Egan, Gerard. *The Skilled Helper*. Monterey, California: Brooks/Cole Publishing, 1982.

Hestenes, Roberta. *Using the Bible in Groups*. Philadelphia: Westminster Press, 1983.

The Ideas Library. 46 Volumes. El Cajon, California: Youth Specialties.

Johnson, David, and Frank Johnson. *Joining Together*. Englewood Cliffs, New Jersey: Prentice-Hall Inc., 1975.

Keiser, Fred. *Good News Q's*. El Cajon, California: Youth Specialties, 1988.

Kunz, Marilyn, and Catherine Schell. *How to Start a Neighborhood Bible Study*. New York: Dobbs Ferry, 1981.

Lead Out., Colorado Springs, Colorado: NavPress, 1974.

Lindquist, Stanley. *Action Helping Skills*. Fresno, California: Link-Care Foundation Press, 1976.

Mallison, John. *Building Small Groups in the Christian Community*. New York: Renewal Publications, 1978.

McNabb, Bill, and Steve Mabry. *Creative Bible Teaching*. El Cajon, California: Youth Specialties, 1989.

Nyquist, James. *Leading Bible Discussions*. Downers Grove, Illinois: InterVarsity Press, 1977.

Powell, John. *Why Am I Afraid to Tell You Who I Am?* Texas: Argus Communications, 1974.

Rice, Wayne. *Up Close and Personal: How To Build Community in Your Youth Group*. El Cajon, California: Youth Specialties/Zondervan, 1989.

Tension Getters and *Tension Getters Two*. El Cajon, California: Youth Specialties/Zondervan, 1981, 1985.

Wald, Oletta. *The Joy of Teaching Discovery Bible Study*. Minneapolis: Augsburg Publishing House, 1976.

Walvoord-Girard, Linda. *Teaching the Bible from the Inside Out*. Elgin, Illinois: David C. Cook, 1978.

See page 24 for more great discussion resources.

PART II
DISCUSSION STARTERS

DISCUSSION STARTERS

Joining in a discussion with a group of kids is one of the great joys of youth ministry. Creating an atmosphere where kids feel free to share their feelings and opinions and where kids can grow in their relationships with others is one of the most rewarding experiences you can have. This book was written to encourage and equip you to experience the joy of a discussion. Of course there are problems, of course there are techniques that can improve your discussion-leading skills, and we have tried to help you with the problems and improve your skills; but the main thing we want this book to do is to show you now easy it is to have great discussions with kids.

This section contains 104 ideas you can use to stimulate discussion. Youth leaders have tried out each idea in actual youth groups, so we know they work. You can use these ideas with confidence. But there is one more point we must make: The most important ingredient for a great discussion is not technique or even great ideas. The most important ingredient for a great discussion is a leader who loves kids and loves God. Your love of kids and of God will cover a multitude of mistakes and deficiencies. If the kids sense you really love them and you really love God they will co-operate and work with you to make your discussions effective and successful. So, don't be intimidated. Take your love of God and kids and use this book to get started experiencing the joy of discussion!!

ADVERTISE-MENTS AND COMMERCIALS

Only Beautiful People Drink Diet Sludge

Motivate young people to discuss and evaluate advertisements by giving each person two or three magazines containing plenty of ads. Also give each person a list of values like the one below, with room beside each value to keep score. Instruct the kids to match magazine ads with the values on their lists. Or your young people can evaluate prime-time TV commercials from a videotape you make. When they see an ad or commercial that appeals to a certain value, they should make a mark beside that value. Here's a sample list:

1. Wealth, luxury, greed
2. Security (no worries)
3. Sexual or physical attractiveness
4. Intelligence
5. Conformity (join the crowd)
6. Freedom (do what you want—no responsibility)
7. Justice, human rights (concern for others)
8. Power, strength
9. Responsibility
10. Ego, pride
11. Status (being looked up to)
12. Escapism
13. Humility, self-sacrifice
14. Self-control
15. Ease, comfort
16. Other:

When everyone has finished, discuss the results by asking questions like these:

1. What kind of values do most advertisements or commercials appeal to?

2. What's really being sold in each ad? What else besides the product itself is being promoted?

3. Is there anything unusual or strange in the ad? If so, why did the advertisers put it there?

4. What sells you on the product?

5. Does this ad make males or females look stupid or used? If so, how?

6. How do certain ads focus on guilt and feelings of inadequacy in us?

7. Why do many car manufacturers use sexy women to advertise their cars? Should they? Why or why not?

8. Why are most commercials aimed at a fifth-grade level?

9. Should commercials and advertisements use sports stars?

10. Are there any products that should not be advertised? If so, which ones?

11. How much of advertising is truth? How much is lies? How can you tell the difference? List the ads and the commercials that lie. List the ones that tell the truth.

12. Should advertisements and commercials contain "fine print"?

13. Have you ever used a product that didn't do what it claimed it could do? If so, what did you do about it? What things can you do when products don't live up to their ads?

14. How do advertisements and commercials affect your value system, if at all?

15. Read Matthew 6:19-33, Romans 12:1-2, and Colossians 3:1-2. What can you do to keep your values and priorities straight?

AFFIRMATION Appreciation Game

For this small-group experience, form groups of five to seven people. Each group sits in a circle around a one member of the group, who sits in a chair in the center. As long as she sits in the center chair, she must remain completely silent. One at a time, each person in the circle tells the person in the center three or four things he appreciates about her. Tell the kids to be honest. Be as deep or as superficial as you like, just don't be phony. Ask them to be specific and speak directly to the person in the center. Continue until all have sat in the center chair and heard their small group's affirmations. Following this experience, discuss the following questions with the entire group:

1. Was it easy to receive these compliments? To give them? Why?

2. Describe how you felt.

3. Did you want to avoid communicating directly with the other person?

4. Did you want to avoid, dismiss, or reject the compliments you received?

5. Did some people in your group find it difficult to follow directions? About sitting in silence for several minutes? About expressing appreciation for another person without adding a put-down? About respecting the rights of others to speak?

6. What things did you learn about yourself from this experience?

Football Stadium

This small-group experience uses the imagery of a football game to help members of the group not only to learn more about each other, but to celebrate each others' gifts and position in the body of Christ. Each person answers to question, "If the Christian life were a football game, where would you fit in and why?" One person, for example, might see herself as sitting on the bench—not very active. Someone else might feel he's a cheerleader, giving encouragement to the team but not participating. Others may identify with the coach, the quarterback, or even an empty seat in the stands. Then allow everyone to visualize where they would like to be in the game and why. You might want to prepare a photograph or drawing of a football stadium with players, coaches, and spectators for each group to use, or perhaps list possible participants in a football event to choose from. Close the experience with a round of affirming prayer for each other.

The Balloon Tribe

Sometimes the best way to approach a topic is to use stories and analogies. The following allegory opens up a good discussion of drinking and substance abuse in a non-threatening way.

After the group has read or heard the story of the Balloon Tribe, divide up into three groups according to the position each student takes toward the story:

Group One: Blowing up balloons is fine, and it's okay to run out of breath and get dizzy if you feel like it.

Group Two: Occasional balloon blowing is okay, but it's morally wrong to get dizzy.

Group Three: Blowing up balloons is wrong at all times.

Have the groups defend their positions, and allow switches if desired.

ALCOHOL AND DRUGS

"The Balloon Tribe"

In a primitive country across the ocean lives a tribe that practices a unique social activity. This is the story of how the activity originated and the effect it had on the tribe. It seems that a short while back, one of the tribe members discovered a stretchy substance that came from a local tree. At first, the tribe didn't think this discovery was very important. However, from that substance one tribe member created what we know as a balloon. The tribe thought it a clever but seemingly useless invention.

One day, however, that same tribe member discovered something interesting about the balloons. After blowing up several of them, he became light-headed and out of breath, experiencing a euphoric, dizzy feeling. When he told the rest of the tribe, everyone immediately wanted to try it. Eventually, as this activity increased, the tribe became divided into four groups: the Dizzy Balloon Blowers, the Occasional Balloon Blowers, the Balloon Blowers for Career or Craft, and the Anti-Balloon Blowers.

The Dizzy Balloon Blowers developed a tolerance to blowing up several very large balloons in a short time—usually in just one evening. This group would get together every week and blow up numerous balloons for many different reasons: Some would do it to get dizzier than the time before, some as a reason to get together with their friends, some because it was a way to relax after a hard day in the jungle, some to celebrate, and some just because they weren't getting along with other tribe members. Each Dizzy felt that his reason for blowing up balloons was worth it, even though he often felt sick and nauseated in the morning and promised never to blow up another balloon.

Now the Occasional Balloon Blowers enjoyed a balloon every once in a while. In fact, when they did join the Dizzies, they would take up a whole evening blowing up just one balloon (which was usually not too large). These tribe members blew up balloons for all the same reasons as the Dizzies, but they carefully avoided having to go through what the Dizzies went through the morning after.

The Balloon Blowers for Career and Craft turned balloon blowing into an art. They only blew up the best balloons, not just any old cheap balloon. In fact, many of this group made their own balloons. And fine balloons they were! It was not long after balloons were discovered that this group started contests and competitions to find the best balloon. They examined balloon shape, size, color, and how well it expanded. Many in this group got so good at making balloons that they went full-time.

On the other side of the jungle were the Anti-Balloon Blowers. They had seen the damage done from blowing up too many balloons and getting dizzy. (Some members of this group were former Dizzies.) They loudly protested that absolutely no one should blow up balloons! Balloon blowing had caused tribal families to break up and hate one another, they said. Many tribe members had given up their tribal responsibilities so they could blow up balloons all day and get dizzy. Some Dizzies got too dizzy to paddle their canoes home and drowned trying to do so.

With the many groups of balloon blowers—and the Anti-Balloon Blowers—it was difficult to assess the overall benefit or detriment to the tribe as a direct result of the balloons. Some members would not touch balloons while some seemingly could not face life without them. In some way every tribe member had to make up his or her mind ◇

Paul's Dilemma

Read aloud or act out the following situation in which a teenager named Paul receives advice from friends and relatives. Use the discussion question at the end of the script to prompt the kids to respond to the story.

The Situation: Paul, a junior in high school, is accepted by his friends, makes average grades, and is a member of several school organizations—choir, the basketball team, and the student council. He has been friends with one group of five guys through most of his junior-high and high-school years. His father is a lawyer, and his mother is the secretary of a popular civic organization. The whole family is active in the local church where his father and mother hold leadership positions.

Paul's problem is this: Although in the past the values of Paul and his five friends have been similar, lately the guys have been experimenting with drugs and alcohol. Paul has participated until now, but he is feeling more and more uncomfortable. He has discussed the problem with his buddies and they're not planning to change. If Paul decides to stop going along with the group, it may cost him his relationship with the guys. He approaches a number of acquaintances seeking advice.

Youth Group Sponsor: He is concerned that Paul may get sucked into the habits of his buddies. Reminding him that Jesus never allowed relationships to get in the way of conviction, he advises Paul to walk away from the friendships. He refers to men like Martin Luther who did what they knew was right regardless of the circumstances.

Paul's Uncle: His favorite uncle, who is also a lawyer, listens nervously as Paul confides that he really doesn't see what's so wrong with all of these things. It's just that he doesn't feel right. Paul's uncle immediately cites statistics that show the dangers of marijuana and alcohol use. He attempts to rationally investigate all of the phony justifications for using grass and alcohol and makes a case for abstinence—the only really logical and safe course.

Sunday School Teacher: He points out that you are either with Christ or against him. You are either committed or not committed. The issue is choosing to behave like a Christian should—renouncing every appearance of evil—or choosing to capitulate to the world and sell out to sin.

Youth Director: He relates to Paul a true story of a close friend who was bothered by the direction his friends were going, but didn't have enough courage to stand for his conviction. The result was that he became heavily involved in drugs, disgraced his family and friends, and eventually committed suicide. He suggests that Paul has great potential to influence hundreds of young people and urges him not to blow his potential over a few foolish friends. In fact, the youth director confides, he was just going to ask Paul to take a leadership position in the group.

A Neighbor (who is also a policeman): He confronts Paul with a report on some of Paul's friends who are on the brink of getting into trouble over drugs. The neighbor is concerned that Paul understand the legal implications of his friends' behavior and counsels him to stay away from them to avoid getting busted. The neighbor goes on to explain that personally he does not see what's wrong with a kid experimenting with marijuana, but that we must all obey the laws or there will be total chaos. Laws are there for our protection and we must follow them.

The Pastor: He points out that the church has always spoken out against non-Christian behavior and that ever since the church was founded such things were not acceptable for church members. The purity of the church, whether it's a local body of believers or the church universal, has always been a focal point of our doctrine.

His Girlfriend: She says not to worry about what anyone else says—he should do what's right. If he makes the wrong choice, he'll never be able to live with himself. She reminds him that if his parents knew he was experimenting with marijuana and alcohol, his mother would be crushed and his father would be humiliated. "Besides," she says, "what about me and our relationship? You know what I think of your group of friends and what they are doing. If I mean very much to you, you better think carefully about what you're doing."

Paul's Older Brother: He thinks Paul is too narrow and is making an issue out of nothing. He feels Paul is experiencing false guilt produced by the unenlightened views of their parents. He argues that he regularly smokes pot and drinks and still maintains a high grade point average and also holds down a good job. He counsels Paul not to get involved in heavy drugs or excessive drinking, but warns him not to sacrifice his good friendships for a non-issue.

Questions for discussion:

1. Evaluate each of the arguments given to Paul. What are the strengths, if any, and what are the weaknesses, if any?

2. Which person do you most agree with? Why? Which one do you least agree with? Why?

3. What answer would you give Paul? What would you do in Paul's situation?

4. Is there a right answer to Paul's dilemma?

5. What were Paul's alternatives?

6. If Paul had weighed all the alternatives and made what you considered a wrong choice, what would you say to Paul if you were:

   a. a close friend
   b. a girlfriend
   c. a parent
   d. a brother/sister
   e. a youth director
   f. a minister
   g. a school counselor

The Mad Photographer

ANGER

Here's a powerful way to get your group hooked into a session on anger. Recruit one young person beforehand to play the role of photographer. From the beginning of the meeting time, the photographer shoots flash pictures of the games, singing, and announcements. You then gently ask him to please stop taking pictures, and repeat this with increasing intensity as he continues to go ahead and take more pictures anyway.

As the serious time of the meeting approaches, you give the photographer one last ultimatum. Then just as you start to speak, he takes one last picture. You react with fury, walk over to the young person, grab the camera and pull out the film, shouting about the previous warnings. The kids will react in a variety of ways. The situation turns around when you walk back to the front and say, "Tonight we are going to discuss handling our emotions. Let's start with anger." Debrief the episode by pointing out the tremendous power of one angry person and the various reactions of the group to the anger that you demonstrated.

Questions for discussion:

1. What makes you angry?

2. What do you do when you get angry?

3. How do you deal with anger?

4. Anger is listed as one of the "Seven Deadly Sins." Is anger a sin? Or is it a normal human emotion?

5. What does the Bible teach about anger?

6. Do Christians express anger differently than non-Christians? If so, how?

APPEARANCE

Mirror, Mirror

The following multiple-choice questionnaire is an excellent discussion starter on the subject of personal appearance. Most kids worry a great deal about how they look, and this questionnaire can help give some direction and substance to this natural preoccupation.

This questionnaire could be combined with other appearance-oriented exercises or crowd breakers for an entire meeting or program on this theme. Here are some suggestions:

1. Start with a fashion show. (Check Youth Specialties' Ideas Library for some crazy ways to do this.)

2. Have a "best dressed" contest. Have kids come up with a list of the 10 best dressed people in the church or the youth group.

3. Hang up some pictures of people with different kinds of appearances (dress, hair, etc.) and have the kids make

My Appearance

Please answer these questions in order. Don't go back and change your answer; your initial response was probably most honest.

1. I think about my appearance...
   □ constantly □ regularly
   □ when it is called to my attention □ rarely
   □ never (even when looking in a mirror)

2. The money I spend on clothes and my appearance is...
   □ ridiculous □ too much
   □ about right □ not enough

3. I dress the way I do for church on Sundays primarily because...
   □ I feel most comfortable this way
   □ it is what others expect
   □ I don't want to be noticed, stick out
   □ I want others to notice me
   □ I think God would be pleased
   □ I was taught by my parents to dress this way
   □ other _____

4. I think the teaching from 1 Corinthians 11:13-16—that long hair is a disgrace for men but a woman's glory and that it's improper for a woman to pray with her head uncovered—is

□ just cultural (to be applied only to the time it was written in)
□ applicable to us today
□ only partly true for today (even though it appears in the same paragraph in the Bible)
□ other _____

5. Quite honestly, I...
   □ judge people on the basis of their appearance
   □ don't let appearance affect the way I think of people
   □ let appearance affect the way I judge people some, and rightly so!
   □ try not to be affected by people's appearance, but I can't help it

6. I dress the way I do at work or school because...
   __ □ I feel most comfortable that way
   __ □ it is what others expect
   __ □ I don't want to be noticed, stick out
   __ □ I want others to notice me
   __ □ because I think God will be pleased
   __ □ I was taught by my parents to dress that way
   __ □ I would lose my job or be kicked out of school if I dressed otherwise
   __ □ other _____

7. Put a number beside each reason listed in question 6 that shows which is the best (1) and which is the worst (7) reason for dressing the way one does—whether you live by that order or not.

8. Most people in our society (culture) are...
   □ hung up on appearance
   □ don't care enough about their appearance
   □ have a good perspective on the importance of appearance
   □ other _____

9. If I could change one thing about my appearance, it would be...

   _____
   _____
   _____

10. The reason I would change what I chose in the previous statement is...
    □ I would impress others more favorably
    □ I would be able to forget about this thing that bothers me a lot
    □ I would be better in sports
    □ I would feel better (physically)
    □ I would be more attractive to the opposite sex
    □ other _____

11. Please rate the following three categories as to whether you think it (1) matters very much to God, (2) matters very little to God, (3) matters to God only if it matters to us, or (4) really doesn't matter at all to God
    __ how I dress
    __ whether I am overweight or underweight
    __ whether I shower, shave, keep my hair combed and cut regularly

12. A Christian in our society...
    □ should have about the same idea about appearance that others in our society do. In other words, there's little wrong with how our society thinks about appearance
    □ should be distinctly different than most of society in the way he thinks about appearance
    □ other _____

13. When I am dressed differently than others in a social situation, I feel...
    □ pleased □ comfortable
    □ embarrassed, conspicuous
    □ other _____

conclusions about the values or lifestyles represented. The object is to determine whether or not there is a connection between outward appearance and the "real" person.

4. Have the youth sponsors dress in a very sloppy or bizarre manner for the meeting. Or just different from normal. Watch the kids' reactions. Or...

5. Encourage the kids to come to the meeting dressed in a different or unusual way. You might have everyone come in formal attire or as sloppy as possible or wearing their favorite clothes.

6. You might have a game or drawing in which the winner gets a gift certificate to a clothing store. (You might be able to get this donated.)

Print enough copies of the following questionnaire to give one to each person. After 10 or 15 minutes of filling it out, lead them to discuss the questionnaire. Focus on principles that teach kids to care about their appearance without being obsessed with conformity or status-seeking and without being phony.

ATTITUDES — Parable of the Plants

Like most parables, this story is most effective when you allow it to make its own point instead of using it to buttress a point that you are trying to get across. Open-ended discussion, however, is appropriate and helpful.

Suggested questions for discussion:

1. Complete this sentence: "The moral of this story is..."

2. Which plant in the story do you most identify with?

3. What kind of person might each plant represent? What attitudes or outlooks on life do you recognize?

4. Which plants are more "Christian"?

5. What Scripture passages apply to this story?

Parable of the Plants

One day a boy named Stu happened to be skipping by an orchard near his home and discovered six small plants all in a nice neat row. He stopped and looked at each one very carefully. How droopy they each looked.

Being a curious and determined little boy, Stu marched up to the first plant and said, "Little plant, what's wrong with you?"

"What's wrong with me?" the plant responded. "Why, nothing! This is the way I'm supposed to look. Surely you can see I'm the same as the others?"

"Well, yes..."

Stu frowned a bit in thought and then walked over to the second plant. "Little plant, what's wrong with you."

"Let me tell you what's wrong!" it said heatedly. "First of all, this is crummy soil. I need an acid pH soil and this is alkaline. I need a place where I can stick my roots down deep, but there's hardpan here. And who can get any sunlight while that big oak tree hogs it? Whoever planted me didn't know what he was doing."

"Hmmm..." said Stu, and strolled over to the third plant. "Little plant, what's wrong with you?"

It pointed its longest, droopiest leaf to the others. "It's their fault. I was here first. I was the first to come up. There was plenty of room for me to grow, plenty of room for just one plant. Then they came. Before you know it, we were arguing. I told them by rights the water belonged to me, but they disagreed. Sure enough,

the water table soon dropped—the summer heat hit us, and it was too late. Now look at us. If they'd only get up and leave my property I know I could make it."

The boy politely thanked him and approached the fourth plant. "Little plant, what's wrong with you?"

But the plant said nothing.

"Little plant, what's wrong with you? Little plant, what's..." Stu stood quite still. Now he realized the plant was dead. He shook his head and walked over to the next plant. "Please, little plant, tell me what's wrong with you."

"Well, it looks tough now," it said stoutly, "but I know I can make it. If I just get a little water from over there and stretch a bit out in the sunlight and grow an angle here, I'll have it licked. I can make it on my own. I don't know about the rest of them, but I'm going to do all it takes to survive. I'll struggle, cut corners, squeeze—no doubt about it, I'll make it!"

"Good for you!" cried Stu. He hummed a snatch of a cheery little tune and then leaned down close to the last little plant. "Now, little plant, what's wrong with you?"

"Water! I need some water," it said matter-of-factly. "But there's no way to get it. Young man, would you be so kind as to fetch me some water and pour it around these parched roots? Then I'll firm up and be healthy and strong."

So, the little boy watered the sixth plant and it grew and grew and grew. ◇

Appendices, Unite!

This game leads into a discussion on the body of Christ or Christian unity. When the group arrives, give everyone a slip of paper with a part of the body on it like ear, nose, foot, kneecap, hand, eye, etc. Distribute enough "parts" to make up

BODY OF CHRIST

two or more complete bodies. In other words, if you have 30 kids, you might want to have three bodies, each with 10 parts.

When the signal to go is given, the kids try to form complete "bodies" as quickly as possible by getting into groups. The body that gets together first is the winner. A complete body has, of course, only one hand, two arms, two legs, and so on. If a body has three legs, one of the legs has to find a different body.

Once the bodies are formed, start some small group discussions or other activities which require those bodies to work together as a team. This simulates how the body of Christ works. An experience like this can help kids to understand passages of Scripture like 1 Corinthians 12 much better.

CHARACTER TRAITS

Building An Image

Here's a learning experience for your youth group which involves role playing and discussion. It focuses on character traits and peer approval.

Divide into small groups that function independently. Give each person the following list of character traits. Everyone reads through the list and assigns a number value to each trait on a scale of 1 (low) to 10 (high).

1 = an absolutely worthless or negative character trait

5 = neither good or bad

10 = essential to a respectable and likeable person

Next, put a batch of role plays in a hat. They can be of any type—crisis resolution, humorous situation, everyday experience. In a different hat put paper slips on which you've written everyone's name. Select one name. That individual is to pick a role play. Then select more names out of the hat to fit whatever other roles are needed for the play.

All the people involved in the role play are to look over their list of character traits and select three that they will use during the role play.

Allow about three minutes for the kids to perform the role play. As they watch the role play, the rest of the group members must attempt to determine (privately) which traits each of the role players is dramatizing. After time is called, the small groups confer to decide which traits were being acted out.

Do several rounds of role playing similarly. The object is to figure out what personality types are most acceptable to the group and to act that way.

Follow up with a discussion using these questions:

1. Which are the most desirable character or personality traits? Why?

2. How can a person develop these traits?

3. Why are these traits so important to your friends?

4. Which coincide with biblical values? Which contradict biblical values?

5. What happens to the kids who go against the flow of their peers' opinions?

Character Traits

___ Critical, fault finding
___ Inquisitive
___ Gullible
___ Spineless
___ Analytical
___ Picky, fussy, over-concerned about details
___ Daydreaming
___ Selfish
___ Competitive
___ Vain, conceited
___ Scheming, conniving, devious
___ Caring
___ Confident
___ Cooperative
___ Compromising
___ Courteous
___ Flattering
___ Decisive
___ Inflexible, one-track mind
___ Funny, joking
___ Impatient
___ Aggressive
___ Energetic
___ Melodramatic
___ Verbose, wordy, talkative
___ Indecisive
___ Patient
___ Big shot
___ Accusing, blaming
___ Frank, outspoken, blunt
___ Insensitive, unloving
___ Grateful
___ Friendly, cordial
___ Apathetic, indifferent
___ Stubborn, inflexible, intolerant
___ Self-critical, self-abasing
___ Pushy
___ Loud
___ Respectful
___ Mocking
___ Cool
___ Sensitive, touchy, easily offended

The Crutch Walkers

CHRISTIANITY

Christianity, some say, is a mere crutch. This parable illustrates that we are all handicapped without Christ, and only when we admit that we are crippled can we begin to learn to walk. Read it to the group and then discuss the questions that follow.

There was once a planet inhabited by beings who could not walk. They crawled through life not knowing the pleasure of viewing life upright nor enjoying the easy mobility of walking. They had not always lived like that, however. History books recorded long ago their ancestors had used their legs effectively and walked upright, not crawling or pulling their bodies along with their hands as they did now.

One day a person came along who showed great love and compassion toward them. He told them that not only had their ancestors walked with their legs, but that this was possible for them too. He offered crutches to those who believed his promise that after using their crutches faithfully, someday they would be able to walk upright even without them.

Some of the people decided to try the crutches. Once they were upright they found how much larger their world became because of this new ease in mobility. They encouraged everyone to join them in this newly found freedom.

Others doubted the crutch walkers would ever be free of their crutches and be able to walk alone. They scoffed at them and said, "We are satisfied with life as we live it. We don't need the assistance of a crutch to experience life. Only the weak need the aid of crutches to get around!"

Questions for discussion:

1. If you were one of the people in the story, would you have tried the crutches? Why or why not?

2. Why do you think some people did not want to try to crutches, and put other people down who did?

3. Do you feel that Christianity is only a crutch? If so, in what way? Is this good or bad?

4. How would you respond to a person who rejected Christianity because he thought that it was "only a crutch"?

Role Bowl

Print up the following situations on cards, and put them in a bowl. Let each person in a small group pick one to read aloud. After the one who picked it offers her solution, allow others in the group to add their thoughts.

1. I don't get it. If Christianity is true, how come there are so many religions that call themselves Christian? I mean, what's the difference between Baptists, Presbyterians, etc?

2. If you ask me, the Christian religion makes you a doormat. It doesn't make sense to be always loving and turning the other cheek.

3. What if I lived like hell for 80 years and then became a Christian on my death bed? Would me and Billy Graham go to the same place?

4. I have been reading through the Old Testament for English class. How come God ordered his people to kill everybody—even women and children—when they conquered a land? What kind of a God is that?

5. Your mother and I do not believe in all this Jesus stuff, and we think you spend too much time in church. So we want you to stay away from church for a while.

6. If God is God, then how come you can't see him or it? Why don't you prove that God exists? Go ahead...prove it to me.

7. The Bible has some nice little stories in it, but everyone knows it's full of contradictions, errors, and just plain myths. How can you believe it?

8. I know a bunch of Christians who go to your church. I also know what they do during the week and at parties I go to. They are phonies. If Christianity is so great, how come there are so many phonies?

9. My little brother died of leukemia, and I prayed like crazy. Don't tell me there is a God who loves us. How come he didn't help my brother?

10. Look, I know I'm overweight and—though it hurts me to say it—ugly. I started coming to your church because I thought the kids in your youth group would treat me differently from the way kids at school treat me. Wrong! The people in your group ignore me or make fun of me just like everyone else. How come?

What, Me a Christian?

The following true-false quiz, "What is a Christian," forces kids to think through some of their own assumptions as well as questions frequently raised by others.

Give each person a copy of this quiz and ask them to circle T or F beside each statement. Then discuss the answers.

What Is a Christian?

T F 1. The only thing one must do to be a Christian is to attend church on Sunday.

T F 2. The only thing one must do to be a Christian is to be a member of a church.

T F 3. A person becomes a Christian when he is baptized.

T F 4. A person becomes a Christian when she is confirmed.

T F 5. In order to be a Christian, you only have to believe that Jesus Christ died for your sins.

T F 6. All real Christians are "Born Again" Christians.

T F 7. Every member of this church is a Christian.

T F 8. Jesus was a Christian.

T F 9. Only those people who belong to the _____ Church are Christians.

T F 10. Most people in my church only say they are Christians, but they really are not Christians.

T F 11. To be a Christian one must read the Bible regularly.

T F 12. Everyone who goes to church is a Christian.

T F 13. All Christians believe the same things.

T F 14. Being a Christian means that I can't do all the fun things that my friends do.

T F 15. One can be a Christian and still believe that drinking alcohol is okay.

T F 16. Once one is a Christian, she never sins again.

T F 17. You can tell that a person is a Christian by the way he acts.

T F 18. Christians do not swear or curse.

T F 19. Christians love everyone.

T F 20. My parents are Christians.

T F 21. As a Christian, I must do the right things in order for God to continue to love me.

T F 22. God loves Christians more than he loves non-Christians.

T F 23. God does not allow Christians to get hurt.

T F 24. Most of my friends are Christians.

T F 25. I am a Christian.

Ideal Church

CHURCH

Give five index cards to each person. Ask everyone to write one completion to the following statement on each card: "The ideal church would be one that..." When the kids finish writing, ask them to order the rejoinders they wrote from 1 (most important) to 5 (least important), mark the rank on the back of the card.

Then open up trading—one for one—where each young person tries to accumulate the five cards they desire most for their ideal church. After some spirited trading, instruct everyone to discard three of the five cards they now possess, keeping the best two. Finally, allow several minutes for the kids to form a "church" consisting of four or five members of the group.

Once divided into churches, each church group should choose a name and, if time permits, design a symbol for their church. Allow each group to present its church to the entire group and to explain its symbol and its goals as a church community.

The Man from Ick

Read the following parable to the group and provide time to discuss its meaning. Sample questions are provided.

Questions for discussion:

1. What does this story mean to you?

2. Is it a legitimate function of the church to protect its people?

3. What things in the church suffocate you? What things in the church are like fresh air?

4. What do you think of church schools, Christian yellow pages, Christian communes?

5. What does it mean to be "in the world, but not of it"?

6. Can you separate from the world without being isolated from the world?

The Man from Ick

Once there was a town called Ick.

The people of Ick had a problem—they were icky.

For some unexplained reason, everyone who was born in Ick ended up icky. Scientists, doctors, experts from all over the world had tried to analyze the people of Ick, and although they all agreed that the people of Ick were icky, no one could agree on a cure. In fact, there was no cure.

The scientists, doctors, and experts agreed that the only thing they could do would be to give people suggestions on how to cope with their ickyness.

But experts or no experts, everyone learned to cope in their own way. Some pretended they weren't icky. Some tried to keep busy and forget their ickyness. Others decided that being icky was better than not being icky...and they got ickier. Some just didn't care. But if you were able to get a person from Ick to be honest, they really didn't like being icky.

Well, you can imagine how many people arrived in Ick with a cure for ickyness. And you can imagine how many people were always willing to try each new cure that came along. And strangely enough, some of the cures seemed to work...for a while. But eventually, the cure would stop working and everyone would be icky again.

One day something happened that radically changed the people of Ick.

A long-time resident of Ick began to suggest publicly that he had a cure for ickyness. It was very difficult for the people of Ick to believe that a person who lived in Ick himself could have a real cure for ickyness.

But then something strange happened. One of the ickiest people in all of Ick believed

in this cure and was changed. He simply wasn't icky anymore. Everyone thought it was just temporary and waited. But it didn't go away, and before long lots and lots of people started believing the man from Ick...and everyone who believed was cured.

It was incredible! And one would think that the people of Ick were overjoyed. But the people weren't overjoyed, and soon a town meeting was called.

The fact of the matter was, the business community of Ick had been built around the basic fact of people's ickyness. And with more and more people losing their ickyness, the economic future of Ick was threatened. After an extremely heated discussion, it was generally agreed that what appeared to be a cure for ickyness was probably like all the other so-called cures and would soon turn out to be a hoax. And since so many people were being misled, and since it was possible that many more people could be misled, and since a person who would perpetuate such a hoax on a community like Ick could affect the stability of Ick, the savior of Ick was asked to leave.

He refused. He continued to cure people, and each day those responsible for the stability of Ick became more and more concerned.

One day, however, the savior of Ick disappeared. It caused quite a commotion, and no one to this day knows what happened. Some said he was done away with. Others said they actually saw him the day after he disappeared. But what was strange was that even though the savior of Ick was gone, people who believed in him and his cure suddenly would find their ickyness gone. And even though the majority of the townspeople were in agreement that this savior was a hoax, all those who believed in him were still cured.

The people who had lost their ickyness thought everyone would jump at the chance to be cured. They were sadly disappointed. Very few were even interested. So the ex-icky people did what they could to convince the icky people that their cure was not a hoax, and every once in a while someone would believe.

Apparently—this is only hearsay—a small group of ex-icky people began to worry that if they or their children associated too much with icky people, they might be contaminated or become icky again.

It wasn't long before these people banded together and moved to the top of Ick Hill, an isolated spot on the edge of town. They worked, shopped and went to school in downtown Ick, and then returned to Ick Hill for their evenings and weekends. But it wasn't long before the people of Ick Hill became so fearful of contamination that they built their own school, market, gas station, and shopping center.

One morning, several months later, the people of Ick woke up to see Ick Hill covered by a large glass bubble. Ick Hill was now a completely self-contained community with everything completely under control.

One particularly cold morning, an icky person in the city of Ick noticed that there was no visible activity going on inside the glass bubble of Ick Hill. A rescue party was sent to see if everything was all right.

After breaking through the glass bubble, they were shocked to find the entire population of Ick Hill dead. Autopsies were ordered, and the cause of death was the same for all.

Suffocation.

Phoenix Game

The following exercise in establishing priorities in the church helps young people determine their own goals and examine their attitudes toward the church.

Print up the following letter (adapted to fit your church), and place it in envelopes addressed to each young person in the youth group.
Have a surprise "mail call" and distribute the letters. Break into small groups and begin planning your new church.

Regroup at a specified time for sharing of organizational charts and discussion. Ask if the suggestions would really work and whether or not they could be incorporated into the present church structure.

The Sermon of the Mouse

Raise some important issues concerning the church by reading the following article aloud to the group or printing enough copies to give one to each person. Discuss answers to the questions that follow.

Dear _____,
As an authorized agent of the Nature Wide Insurance Company, it is my duty to inform you that at approximately 11 p.m. Friday evening, your pastor, Rev. ____ called all the members of your church together for a special prayer meeting. It is my unhappy duty to also inform you that at 11:10 the Air Force accidentally dropped a limited-scale nuclear bomb on the church meeting and completely destroyed the church building and Harry's Bar across the street. Harry wasn't in the bar at the time, so he will be able to rebuild his bar. But you and the members of your small group will have to make some vital decisions.

You are the only surviving members of your church, and this makes you legally responsible. There is an insurance policy on the building and grounds for approximately one and a half million dollars that will be paid out to you when you present an organizational chart of what is now your church. As there are no ministers available from denominational headquarters, you will have to provide your own leadership in determining your church structure.

I wonder whether you will want to hire other people to do the work in the church or whether you will do it yourselves. I wonder whether you will pay salaries to yourselves. I expect you to build a new building, will you? What will it look like?

These are all questions that must be answered in the near future. For now, please complete these forms so that we can settle your insurance claims as quickly and easily as possible. Thank you. Good luck!
1. `What is name of your church? (Will you keep the name ____ or will you change it?)
2. Who are the leaders in your church, and what are their roles and salaries, if any?
NAME _____
CHURCH JOB _____
SALARY_____
3. On the other side of this page, make an organizational chart of your church.
4. Describe briefly the type of building you plan to construct or your reasons for not having a building (you don't need a building to receive the insurance reimbursement).
5. Describe your new church's type of ministry? What is your basic purpose?

The Sermon of the Mouse

The day had finally arrived. Everyone in the congregation was waiting expectantly. The negotiations had taken months, but finally everything had been worked out. It wasn't every congregation in the country that could have an opportunity like this. It was a rare visit from a very well known celebrity.

The pastor and his guest mounted the platform. The first hymn was sung. Then the pastor rose. "I'm sure everyone knows who our guest speaker is this morning," he said.

How could anyone help but know? Posters all over town announced his coming. A big yellow and black banner stretched across the entry to the parking lot. Seating in the sanctuary had been done on a reservation basis with preferential treatment given to members in good standing. An overflow crowd was watching the service on closed circuit television. Everybody knew about it.

"It isn't often," said the pastor, "that we have an opportunity to meet someone who has become a legend in his own time. Starting back in the bleak years of the depression with a shoe-string budget and a very simple plan, our guest, with hard work and contagious enthusiasm, built an empire for himself that rivals that of Howard Hughes. His name is a household word. He is admired by young and old alike. He has even survived his mentor. He reigns over a multi-million dollar business venture that was so successful in southern California that he established an even more spectacular venture in Florida. By now I'm sure you know who I am talking about. We are so honored to have Mickey Mouse with us today to share with us the secrets of Disneyland's success, with the hope that our church will be stimulated and helped by his story."

A hush came over the congregation as this famous mouse rose to his feet, cleared his throat, and began his sermon.

"Thank you for inviting me to come to your church. I must admit, at first I was surprised that a church would ask me to give a sermon. Oh, I've been invited to Sunday school contests where they give each new person a Mickey Mouse hat and expect me to shake hands with everyone and act funny. But a sermon is something new.

"But after I thought about it, I realized that maybe Disneyland and the Church do have a lot in common. And as I began to organize my thoughts, I saw how ingenious it was to invite me to share. I really believe that if your church were to apply our principles, you could become as successful as Disneyland.

"First, make sure your enterprise seems exciting, even dangerous—but be quick to let your people know that there really is no danger involved. Give the illusion of great risk, but make sure everything is perfectly safe.

"Second, admit that you are in the entertainment business. People won't care what you say as long as they're entertained. Keep your people happy. Don't tell them anything negative. And don't make demands on them. Just keep them diverted from the ugly reality of today's world, and they will keep coming back for more.

"Third, make everything look religious. Make the religious experience so intricate, so complex that only the professionals can pull it off while all the laymen stand around watching with their mouths open. Just as people would rather pay to watch a mechanical bird sing on cue, so they would rather watch an elaborate worship than participate in worshipping.

"Fourth and finally, pretend that there are no problems. At Disneyland we dress our security guards up as smiling rabbits or friendly bears because we don't want anyone's experience at Disneyland to be ruined by the sight of law enforcement personnel. Disguise your problems behind a warm smile and a firm handshake. Leave troubles at home, and let the church be a happy place of friendly pastors and smiling deacons.

"People today want good clean entertainment and they want an environment that is safe for children, family, and friends. I am so glad to see that the church is moving in this direction. Thank you, and God bless you."

Questions for discussion:

1. What parallels, if any, do you see between Disneyland and the organized church?

2. Analyze each of the mouse's points. Below are some questions that may help:

■ "Give the illusion of great risk, but make everything safe."

a. Are there any risks involved in being a Christian today?

b. Does modern Christianity really cost the Christian anything?

c. Can you think of any examples of the church creating an illusion of risk?

d. How, if at all, does a church give people safety?

■ "Entertain the people."

a. How do churches entertain their people?

b. Should Christianity and the church be entertaining?

c. React to this statement: "People today must be entertained. After watching sophisticated, professional entertainment on television and at the movies, people need to feel it's worth their time and attention to come. Of course, the content will be spiritual."

■ "Make everything look religious."

a. Define religious.

b. What do you think Mickey Mouse meant by religious?

■ "Pretend there are no problems."

a. Do you think the church should admit to having problems? The pastor? The people?

b. How can a church pretend it doesn't have any problems?

c. If Christianity is true, then don't problems raise doubts in the minds of searching unbelievers?

CLIQUES — Loving the Unlovely

In this role play Joe Director (leader of the youth group), Grungy Gertrude (wearing dirty, unmatched, out-of-style clothing), and Mod Mary (wearing fashionable clothing, pretty) demonstrate a cliquish attitude at work in a youth group.

Joe is preparing the room for the youth meeting to start when Grungy Gertrude walks in. Joe says hello curtly while continuing to busily set up chairs, etc. She follows him around relentlessly, telling him about her day—she got a "D" in Home Ec, went to a worm wrestle after school, lost a chess tournament, got to buy lunch at school instead of taking a sack. Joe is cold.

Mod Mary arrives. Joe meets her with a big smile and handshake. He asks her questions and listens sympathetically. He invites her to have dinner with his family that week. Gertrude tries to join in the conversation, but no one acknowledges her. Mary sits down. Gertrude looks for a seat, but they are all taken. Joe suggests that she sit on the floor on the far end of the circle. Joe and Mary enthusiastically start singing, "We are one in the Spirit." Gertrude sits with a dejected, puzzled look on her face.

Lead the group to discuss their response to the role play by asking these questions: How did they feel toward Joe, Gertrude and Mary? Did anyone identify with one of the characters? How could each person have acted differently? What would Jesus have done? Have you seen this type of behavior in our group? What can you personally do to prevent it?

Turn to James 2:1-13 and 1 Samuel 16:7. Discuss the principles of love at work in these passages.

People Puzzle Groups

For the following experiment in communication, divide your large group into groups of five. (Pick helpers if there are people left over—the ones you think would get the least out of the experiment.) Each person in each group of five receives an envelope containing different shapes of the same color. Use construction paper to make shapes out of these colors: red, blue, black, yellow, green (see instructions below). Each envelope contains shapes in one of these colors. The object is for each group to form five rectangles, all of equal length and width, using the pieces from all the envelopes in that particular group. There are three steps in putting together the puzzles:

1. No speaking. The only thing you can do is offer one of your pieces of the puzzle to a member of your group. You cannot indicate your need for a particular piece. You may only take a piece if it is offered to you (5-10 minutes).

2. No speaking. You can now, however, indicate your need for a particular piece (5-10 minutes).

3. You may speak.

4. (optional) You may help another group finish.

After all the groups have completed their puzzles (allow from 20-30 minutes) discuss the communication and competition that took place during the experiment. Ask the kids to explain how they felt throughout the experiment.

a. How did you feel when you couldn't talk? Did others help you? Why was communication in your group hard (or easy)?

b. How did you feel about the others in your group? Were they selfish or generous? Do you consider yourself generous or selfish?

c. When your group finished were you proud? When did you start competing with other groups? (This always happens—but never use the words team or competition, always group and experiment.)

d. How did you feel when another group wanted to help you? Did you like the other groups, or did you feel they were showing off? Which was the best group? The worst group? Why?

e. How did you feel about yourself, your motives? How do you feel about your ability to communicate? Man's ability to communicate?

The discussion can go many directions. You could end up in a discussion of God's communication to man—why it is so difficult, why he had to become a man to communicate! Or you could end up talking about man's selfishness, pride, or competitive nature. Let your group's interaction steer your choices of discussion topics.

How to make the puzzles

When each group has finished, it will have five rectangles made by piecing the colors together as follows:

To prepare envelopes, cut the shapes at left from the designated colors of construction paper. Make sure they form the five rectangles. Then put all the reds in one envelope, all the blues in another, etc. These five envelopes make up enough for one group. If you have five groups of five people, for example, you'll need 25 envelopes divided so that each of five groups can complete five rectangles of five different colors.

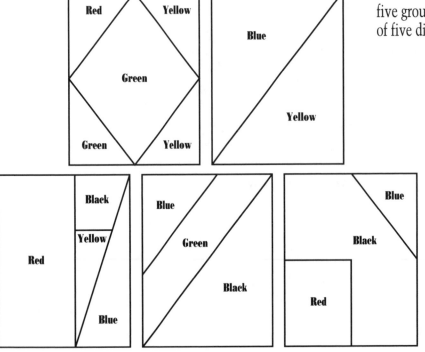

Living Together

Using Acts 2:44-47 as a model, allow the group to explore what the ideal community-living situation would be for our culture today. Divide into small groups and attempt to cover these areas:

1. Living quarters. Should there be separate living quarters for each person? Family unit? Or one large facility shared by everyone?

2. Meals. Will everyone eat together? Separately? What about scheduling?

3. Food. Should it be bought? Grown? Include meat? Vegetables only?

4. Income. Should the group support itself through a cooperative venture or each hold individual jobs and pool money? What about a budget? Allotments or allowances to each member?

5. Location. Should you locate in the city? Suburbs? Woods? Farm? Mountains? Another country?

6. Decisions. Will the group be governed by a leader, committee, the whole group, or elected officials?

7. Rules. Will there be any? If so, what will be the important ones?

8. Maintenance. Who will be responsible for upkeep, repairs, "dirty work"?

9. Children. How will they be cared for? How many allowed? What about education?

10. Standard of Living. Will you "just get by"? Live in poverty? Live comfortably? Try to do as well as you can?

11. Entrance Requirements. Who will you let into the group? Christians only? Certain age groups? Disabled? Elderly? Teens? Wealthy?

12. Habits. Will smoking, drinking, or drugs be allowed? What about personal hygiene and cleanliness—will you let sloppy or irresponsible people join?

13. Religion. Will you all attend the same church? Different churches? Start your own? Attend none?

14. Law. What about marriage? Taxes?

15. Possessions. Will members be able to keep their possessions? Pool them? What about personal items like cars? Stereos? Toothpaste? Clothing?

Have the groups compare their models and try to agree on one ideal community living situation. If you can't agree, isolate the areas of disagreement and discuss why you were unable to compromise.

Discuss your final model in light of the Scriptural model. Discuss the advantages (if any) and disadvantages (if any) of communal living.

Uppers and Downers

For an excellent exercise in community building, have the kids in your group fill out a chart similar to the one below.

Ask the kids to think of a time when someone said something to them that was really a "downer"—something that made them feel bad. This could be a

OTHERS		ME	
UPPER	DOWNER	UPPER	DOWNER

put-down, an angry comment, anything. Then have them think of a time when someone said an "upper" to them—something that made them feel good. If they can think of several entries for the first two columns, encourage them to write them in.

Next, in the third and fourth columns, ask the kids to record times when they said an upper or downer to someone else.

If your kids are typical, chances are they will think of many more downers than uppers. Discuss what this means. Talk about how easy it is to discourage or put others down without a second thought—how damaging our tongues can be, and how the damage takes so long to repair.

Follow up with a look at Hebrews 10:23-25, which deals with encouragement, and then discuss practical ways to put it into practice. Encourage your young people to be more careful about what they say by identifying the words they say to each other as uppers or downers. If you are on a weekend retreat, challenge them to confront each other during the retreat when they hear someone giving someone else a downer. This can cut down on the negativism that often ruins youth group meetings and activities.

Alien from Zipstuck

Ever wonder what someone from a radically different culture would think about our culture? Divide into groups of three or four people. Give each group a stack of magazines and newspapers (magazines heavy on advertisements and photos work best). Ask each group to pretend that they're from the planet Zipstuck. Their assignment is to return to Zipstuck with a report on what the Earthlings are like. Since they don't know our language, their reports must be made up totally of advertisements and pictures.

Each group then tears out the advertisements and photos and develops a brief presentation for the Big Zipper on what the Earthlings are like, based on the ads and photos.

Get ready for a hilarious and poignant comment on our priorities and our style of living.

Questions for discussion:

1. Okay, Zipstucksters, what do you think about these Earthlings?

2. What appears to be important to them?

3. Based on this information, what is a typical Earthling like?

4. What things do Earthlings value?

5. What does the Bible say about what a person should value?

Dating Data

This idea provides a good opportunity for young people to express their values and opinions about dating in a relaxed and natural way. Place the following assignments around the room, providing blank paper, felt-tip markers, and resource materials at each station. Ask the young people to choose and complete as many assignments as possible in the time allowed. They may work together in small groups or individually. At the end of the period, call for reports and discuss the findings.

Assignments:

1. Write a plan for two people who like each other to get together.

2. Devise a fool-proof method for deciding the difference between love and infatuation.

3. List at least 20 fun things to do on a date. Each must cost less than $10.00.

4. List five guidelines for making a date successful.

5. What advice would you give a Christian who has a crush on a non-Christian? Include the pros and cons of dating a non-Christian.

6. Write a plan for breaking up in the least painful and most healthy way.

7. List the number of people you tell about your dates, and write out 10 pros and cons for talking about your date.

Questions for discussion:

1. Why do some people seem to date "below" themselves—that is, put up with anger, being used, disrespect, etc.?

2. Why do some young people find romance earlier than others?

3. How can we be more comfortable on dates?

4. Should girls ask guys out?

5. Why do some people like to exaggerate what happened on a date?

Dating Round Robin

To get the kids talking about dating, try this idea. Have the group sit in a circle. Go around the circle, giving each person 10 seconds to come up with an idea for a cheap date in their town. If they can't think of one, they are eliminated from the game, and you go on to the next person. Continue playing until only one person is left, or until a specified time limit has been reached. In the church where this game was originated, 12 young people came up with 82 ideas!

Here are some examples:
Go swimming
Go to the zoo
Go get a pizza

Work in a garden together
Make popcorn
Listen to a record
Walk a dog
Cook a meal together
Help an old person
Draw or paint
Talk
Run errands for someone
Play tennis
Have a pillow fight
Visit someone in a hospital
Go on a picnic
Wash the car

Go shopping
Take a train or bus ride
Go to a ball game
Go to a movie
Go to a museum

When the game is over, have the group choose the best ideas or rank the list from most expensive to least expensive, or from best to worst. Follow up with a discussion on what makes a good date. Photocopy your list of ideas and give it to the group as a resource for future dating.

Parent Panel

This transgenerational exercise gives your youth group an opportunity to understand a parent's point of view. Although this particular idea deals with the subject of dating, any subject could be used by following the guidelines given below.

Choose two moms and two dads to be the panelists. (Caution: Do not choose parents who are related to anyone in your youth group. Do not place a husband and wife on the same panel. And be sure the panelists are parents whose children have already passed the dating stage.

About two weeks before the scheduled panel discussion, have your youth group anonymously submit questions about dating. Preview the questions, eliminating duplicates and rewording poorly stated questions. Prepare a master list of questions to duplicate and send it to each panelist a week in advance. On the night of the panel, give each of the young people a copy so they can follow along and take notes.

The leader moderates the panel, going through question by question, then opening the discussion to the entire group.

DEATH Death Fantasy

Here is a list of discussion questions that can help young people express their feelings about death and dying. By using fantasy or make believe, young people often surface their hidden or subconscious feelings about death. This can be either a written quiz or a discussion.

1. How do you most frequently see yourself dying?

2. Who died the way you expect to die?

3. What, to you, would be the worst possible way to die? The best possible way?

4. What habits or characteristics of your life may influence the way you die?

5. When do you think you will die? When would you like to die?

6. What is your dominant attitude or feeling about death (defiance, acceptance, fear, longing, curiosity, avoidance)?

7. Imagine you died yesterday. What would things be like for you?

8. What are you doing now to lengthen your life. Shorten your life?

9. What do you want to accomplish before you die?

10. Describe how you reacted to the death of someone you knew. Did you feel anger, fear, relief, sorrow, pity, frustration?

11. Whose death would bring you the greatest sorrow? The greatest pleasure?

12. Who would care the most if you died? What would they do?

13. Describe your funeral.

14. What would you want inscribed on your tombstone?

Death Walk

Arm the kids with a pencil and small tablet and take them to a local cemetery. Spend 15-20 minutes walking around reading the tombstones or plaques and taking notes on what they find interesting. Come back to the church and discuss what the group read. Discuss the subject of death as it relates to Christian and non-Christian people. Try to decide the person's philosophy of life from what was written on their grave.

Ask these questions:

■ What interesting things did you find?

■ Which tombstone or tombstone saying did you like best? Why?

■ What were some of the people's philosophies of life, based on their tombstones?

■ How did it feel to spend so much time in a cemetery? Why do you suppose you felt that way?

■ Why do you think cemeteries are creepy and scary to most people?

■ Why is death so frightening?

Run for Your Life

Although this discussion deals with death, it is really about life and how we live it. The purpose of this exercise is to help young people evaluate their priorities in light of what is really important. It allows the group to contrast what they are doing now with what they would do if they only had one month to live. Give each person in the group a list similar to the one below:

If I only had one month to live, I would:

1. Perform some high risk feat that I have always wanted to do, figuring that

if I don't make it, it won't really matter.

2. Stage an incredible robbery for a large amount of money, which I would immediately give to the needy and starving of the world.

3. Not tell anyone.

4. Use my dilemma to present the gospel to as many people as I could.

5. Spend all my time in prayer and Bible reading.

6. Make my own funeral arrangements.

7. Offer myself to science or medicine to be used for experiments that might have fatal results.

8. Have as much fun as possible (sex, parties, booze, whatever turns me on.)

9. Travel around the world and see as much as possible.

10. Buy lots of stuff I've always wanted on credit—expensive cars, fancy clothes, exotic food, etc. ("Sorry, the deceased left no forwarding address.")

11. Spend my last month with my family or close personal friends.

12. Not do anything much different. Just go on as always.

13. Isolate myself from everyone—find a remote place and meditate.

14. Write a book about my life (or last month).

15. Sell all my possessions and give the money to my family, friends, or others who need it.

16. Try to accomplish as many worthwhile projects as possible.

17. Other:

Have the group rank these alternatives (plus any they wish to add) from first to last choice. The first item on their list would be the one they would probably do, and the last would be the one they would probably not do. (Another way to evaluate the alternatives is to put each one on a continuum. On one end of the continuum would be "Yes, definitely" and on the other end, "Absolutely not.") Invite everyone to explain their choices and tell why they chose the way that way; then discuss the results with the entire group.

Continuum: Cleaning Up Your Act

For a lively discussion on a variety of topics, have your group decide whether they agree or disagree with the following 12 statements. Type the statements on a sheet of paper with an agree/disagree continuum for the kids to mark their positions (see example).

When they have chosen their positions on each statement, ask the kids to defend their positions in a group discussion. It is wise for you as leader to think through your own position on each statement ahead of time. In addition choose Scripture passages that shed some light on the issues being discussed.

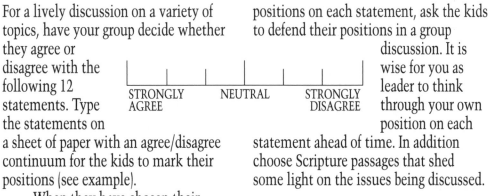

STRONGLY AGREE   NEUTRAL   STRONGLY DISAGREE

1. Pigging out is as wrong as smoking or drinking.

2. While you were walking home one night, a thief jumped from the shadows and demanded all your money. You gave your wallet to the man. He looked in the wallet and asked, "Is this all the money you have on you?" You said, "Yes," and the thief left with bitter threats. You had lied to the man; you had $20 tucked away in your shirt pocket. Was that wrong?

3. To goof off on your job is as wrong as stealing money from your boss.

4. There are degrees of sin with God, so he doesn't really sweat the little sins we commit.

5. As Christians we are to obey all people who are in a position of authority over us, including police officers, parents, and teachers.

6. Your family is late for church, so instead of driving at the 40 mph speed limit, your dad drives at 55. Because you are rushing to a worship service, this is not wrong.

7. Going into your history final, you're just squeezing by with a C. Passing or failing this test could mean the difference between passing or failing the course. During the test you get a few answers from a friend's paper. As you walk out after the test you know you have failed. In this case it is not necessary to confess cheating to the teacher.

8. God made man and woman for each other. God has also created some very attractive bodies. It's okay to lust after someone you see because actually you're just admiring God's creation.

9. A girl is very much in love with her boyfriend, and he has said he loves her so much he would like to marry her eventually. Because she's in love and expects to marry this boy, her body belongs to him for the asking.

10. There is a guy at school who really gets on your nerves. Every time you see him you could punch his lights out. In fact, sometimes you wish he didn't exist. The bitterness you have for this guy is as sinful as if you actually killed him.

11. God doesn't exactly expect you to live as much like Jesus at home as outside the home. After all, we are supposed to be witnesses to all the world, not to our own family.

12. Jesus whipped the money-changers in the temple and chased them out. So it's okay to be obnoxious or cruel if the other person deserves it.

Groupers

Groupers are unfinished sentences such as "I wish I were..." that can be used to stimulate discussion. Through Groupers, young people can express and explore their beliefs and goals and as a result discover what their values really are. Here's one way to use Groupers.

1. Give each person in the group a pencil and paper (golf pencils and index cards work great).

2. State the Grouper aloud to the group, write it on the blackboard, or print it up ahead of time.

3. Emphasize that there are no restrictions on the content of the completed sentences other than that they should be as honest as possible. The emphasis is on spontaneous, true reflections and not on right or wrong answers. No answer is unacceptable. Each person has the right to pass. All answers are anonymous.

4. After everyone completes his Grouper and folds it in half, collect the cards and read them back one at a time.

5. The group can discuss each answer separately or wait until all finished Groupers have been read.

6. Conclude the discussion by reading your own completed Grouper and telling why you responded as you did. Or you may prefer to comment on some of the answers given by the group and introduce some content. (Example: "I was surprised how many of you responded to the statement, 'I fear most...' with the words 'being alone.' Surprisingly, loneliness was a common dilemma of many people in the Bible. Let's take a look...")

Another way to use Groupers is to allow each person to read aloud her completed Grouper. This works best if the members of the group know each other well, and if there is an atmosphere of freedom and trust among group members. Each person can explain his answer and respond, if he chooses, to questions from the group. Every answer is acceptable, and each person has the right to pass.

Below are sample Groupers. While there are many excellent ones here, don't limit yourself entirely to them. These can be a guide for designing Groupers suited the topic you wish to discuss.

1. I fear most...
2. I wish I were...
3. I wish I were not...

4. I wish I had...
5. I wish I had not...
6. I wish I could...
7. If I were President, I would...
8. The President should...
9. The happiest day of my life was...
10. If I could start this year over, I would...
11. My favorite place is...
12. My parents should...
13. I wish my parents wouldn't...
14. What hurts me the most is...
15. If I had $25, I would...
16. I would like to tell my best friend...
17. The worst thing a person could do is...
18. What always makes me mad is...
19. If I could do anything, and no one else would know, I would...
20. I always cry when...
21. I always laugh when...
22. I hate...
23. If I were principal of my school, I would...
24. If I had a million dollars, I would...
25. If my parents left me alone, I would...

"If" Survey

Surveys are excellent ways to stimulate discussion. Either print the following survey for kids to write their responses or ask the questions aloud to open discussion. Follow up with a lesson on self-acceptance, happiness, or God's will.

1. If you could live in any period of history, when would it be? Why?

2. If you could go anywhere in the world, where would you go? Why?

3. If I gave you $3,000, what would you spend it on? Why?

4. If you could change anything about yourself, what would you change? Why?

5. If you could be someone else, who would you be? Why?

6. If you could have any question answered, what would it be?

No-Risk Discussion

If the people in your group seem uneasy about discussing things together, try this no-risk discussion.

Ask questions that require short answers. Ask them one at a time. Each person writes a "1" at the top of a sheet of paper and answers the first question. She then folds the paper down to conceal the answer. After that, she passes the paper to the person on her left. Then each person answers question "2" just below the folded-down portion. With each question, the paper gets folded and passed to a new person till all of the questions have been answered. Collect the papers and redistribute them. Have everyone unfold the paper they receive. As you repeat the questions each person answers the way their paper reads. Doing this activity once or twice helps young people realize that they share the same views with other kids in the group.

Personalized Passages

A great way to get kids more involved in Bible passages is to personalize them. Prepare sentence starters ahead of time that each person must complete in writing or in small-group discussion. The following is a sample from Proverbs, Chapter 10:

1. 10:13) My friends think I'm wise because...

2. (10:14) I get into trouble when I talk too much about...

3. (10:15) One good thing about having lots of money is...

4. (10:15) One good thing about having very little money is...

5. (10:16) If someone gave me $100, I would...

6. (10:16) If I had $10 to spend at the shopping center, I would...

7. (10:19) I feel I have important things to say about...

8. (10:20) People don't listen when I...

9. (10:23) Something that some people consider fun but I don't is...

10. (10:24) I am afraid of...

11. (10:24) My greatest hope is that...

By using phrases like these, you'll help people respond to verses that might otherwise have held no meaning for them. Base the phrases on modern translations for added meaning (those above are from the "Living Bible").

Record Session

Invite kids to bring their favorite records, tapes, or CDs (depending on the sound system you can use). Make a list of one favorite per student without letting anyone know another's choice. Then play a song while everyone tries to guess whose favorite it is. After the song, the person who chose it tells why it is his favorite. Discuss the music style or lyrics if it is appropriate.

After discussing each student's favorite song, try the following meditation experience: Ask the kids to relax, close their eyes, and listen to one last song. As they listen they are to visualize the first scene that pops into their minds and then build a fantasy that grows out of the music. A selection with several contrasting musical experiences carries a fantasy a long way. When the music ends, everyone shares their fantasy. It may develop into a story, the original scene may change, or several scenes may shift back and forth. The important thing is to let the fantasy flow with the music.

Relay Discussion

Set up two, three, or four chairs (no more) in front of your group. Select a person to sit in each chair. Explain that in a relay discussion only the people in the chairs up front can speak; everyone else listens.

To start the kids talking, read aloud agree/disagree statements or statements that beg debate or discussion. The people up front begin discussing your statement (if the kids are shy, ask one of them by name to state her opinion). If a speaker doesn't want to discuss an issue, he may tap the shoulder of anyone in the audience, signaling that person to take his place up front. If someone in the audience wants to respond to the discussion, she may run up front and replace any person there. *Only the people in the front chairs may speak!*

When you sense the discussion slowing down, throw out a new statement. Or stimulate give-and-take by assigning different points of view to the speakers or labeling certain chairs "agree" and "disagree." Here are some sample discussion statements:

1. Jesus identified more with the lifestyle of the poor than the rich; therefore, poor people make better Christians.

2. The reason a church runs a youth program is to prove to itself that it is doing something for young people.

3. A Christian should obey his government, even if it violates the authority of the Scripture.

4. The decision to abort should be left to the parents or parent of the fetus.

5. Bad language is cultural and is thus not un-Christian.

6. Physical violence can be justified by a Christian if it is in self-defense.

7. It is wrong for a Christian to drink alcoholic beverages.

8. Christianity is the only religion through which a person can get to heaven.

9. Our parents discipline us because they are trying to do what is best for us.

Rug Discussion

Here's a great idea to use when you just don't have time to plan your usual terrific youth meeting. It's simple and works like a program that you've spent hours designing.

Pass out 3 x 5 cards to everyone in the room. Suggest a topic for each of the kids to write a question about. Or open the theme to questions about anything that bothers them or that they're struggling with in their lives or that they were just wondering about. Cards should not be signed.

As the kids finish writing out their questions (one per card), they toss them into the center of the discussion circle. Ask someone to draw a question and read it aloud to open discussion. Kids often suggest helpful and honest answers when the question is anonymous.

Tape Talk

One of the best ways to get discussion going in a youth group is to bring in various points of view on a subject. Try interviewing people outside of the youth group on tape and playing it for your youth group. If the subject is "What is love?" for example, interview an engaged couple, a few young children, an elderly widow, a couple married 50 years, someone who's homeless, a mother, or a teacher. After editing out the bad or dull interviews, play the cassette to your group and ask for their reactions, thoughts, and opinions.

Yarn-Sharing Experience

In order to get your group to talk about their inner feelings, try using this technique. Ask the kids to stand in a circle. Pick up a ball of yarn (the size of the ball depends on the size of your group), and explain to the group that they are going to take part in a little experiment. Tell them that in a moment you are going to throw the ball of yarn (while holding on to the end so the yarn will unwind) to someone in the group. When that person catches the ball of yarn, he should talk about one of the following:

1. What God has done for him

2. What God has done for someone he knows

3. What God has done for all of us (Christ's death, given us his Word, etc.)

4. Something she is thankful for

After talking about one of the above, she will throw the ball to someone else in the circle (while holding onto the yarn). The next person who catches the ball will also talk about one of the four things above. Keep this going until everyone in the group has had a chance to talk at least once (several times is best, but this depends on the size of your group and the time you have).

After you have made a web-like pattern with the yarn and everyone has had a chance to share, stop the ball and talk about what's happening.

1. What is this yarn doing for us physically? Answers will range around the idea of "holding us together." (Comment on the beautiful effect the sharing has created, and mention that for the pattern to evolve, everybody had to participate.)

2. Ask one or two members of the group to drop their hold of the yarn. Immediately the center web becomes loose and the effect is for the circle to widen a little. Then ask, "What happens to the group when someone drops their yarn?" (Mention that in talking about their feelings, a beautiful network of relationships and ties were formed—just like the yarn illustrates—but that it takes everyone to hold it together.)

Euthanasia on Trial

This mock trial raises a timely and difficult issue that the entire youth group must discuss as it relates to the three specific cases that the jury decides.

The setting is a hearing on the issue of Euthanasia. (This approach could work with any sticky issue.) Designate part of the youth group as the jury, part as courtroom observers, and part as family members in the three cases described. Choose youth sponsors or articulate young people as lawyers, and the youth minister or another sponsor as the judge. (The "judge" must acquaint himself thoroughly with the issue along with portions of Scripture that are applicable.)

The lawyers' jobs are to present convincing cases for the pro and con side of the choices in each situation, using whatever sources they can find to prove their argument. They can also call witnesses (youth group members who represent family members in the cases described) to bolster their cases. Of course, there should be opportunity for cross examination.

After both sides of all cases have been presented and summary statements made, the jury adjourns to vote on the cases and submit the results to the judge to read to the courtroom. The jury is not deciding whether euthanasia is right or wrong, only whether the individuals in cases A, B, and C should be mercifully put to death. (The jury should decide the cases with little discussion, saving discussion for the entire group to participate in.)

The entire group then discusses the decisions. As judge you wrap up the discussion by reading relevant biblical passages without commenting on their application to the conclusions the kids reached. Let the young people go home and struggle further with their decisions.

Cases for the Jury to Consider:

Case 1: Hortense is a severely retarded, 19-year-old girl. She has control of her muscles, but seems to be around the age of one or two mentally. Through nearly eight years of therapy, doctors and aides have taught her to button the buttons on her clothes. The method they used was much like the method a dog trainer would use to teach a dog tricks: stimulus-response. She might be able to be trained to hold down some extremely simple job on a factory production line, but it would take years to train her. Those years would take large amounts of money both from taxpayers and family, in addition it would take precious time from a doctor or psychiatrist who could be spending his time on someone who was more promising. The family of this patient has asked that they be released from any legal holdings on Hortense, or if that is not possible, that she be mercifully put to death. The jury must decide.

Case 2: Alex is a successful 47-year-old businessman. He went to the doctor for a routine check-up, and the doctor found a large lump in the middle of Alex's back. A biopsy revealed malignant cancer. Radiation therapy was unsuccessful. Now, a month later, Alex is in the hospital in a coma. Doctors believe that he won't live past six months, but he could be given medication (morphine) to lessen the pain. He would have to remain in the Intensive Care Ward till death ($1000/day), and the family would have to bear the cost of doctor bills and medications totaling thousands of dollars. The family could bear the expense, but they cannot bear to see the Alex in constant pain. They ask the doctors either to give Alex a lethal dose of morphine or discontinue all medications and care and let him die naturally and, they hope, quickly. The jury must decide.

Case 3: John and Jane Doe tried for a long time to have children, and when their baby was born, they were eager to take it home. The shape of the baby's head bothered a couple of doctors, however, who ran routine tests to test the baby's brain waves. It turned out that the child suffered severe brain damage during delivery when its skull contracted too tightly around the brain. The child will be a complete idiot mentally. John and Jane left the baby in intensive care while they went home to think the whole matter over. They are just a young couple without financial resources to institutionalize the child. They decide to ask the doctor if the child could be allowed to die. The jury must decide.

Lawyer's Case Against Euthanasia

1. Euthanasia could easily be misunderstood as a recommendation of suicide or of murder of aged or infirm people.

2. How could a weak and/or unbalanced mind, incapable of understanding the conditions, which may be held to render death more desirable than life, make this momentous decision? Case in point: One

highly publicized miraculous cure involved a clergyman's wife who, in a widely circulated letter, had begged that out of "scientific kindness" her physicians terminate her suffering by giving her painless death. Many laymen supported her arguments, but the physicians ignored them and succeeded in restoring her health. She rejoiced that her pleas were disregarded.

3. Who will determine who is to die and how?

4. Putting to death infants with idiocy, retardation, or complete body disfigurement under a Euthanasia Law is belated abortion and a degrading of morality.

5. One alternative is segregation and special training instead of Euthanasia. For example, the feeble minded can be made actually useful, as many of them have considerable physical skills, and they seem to be happy under such conditions.

6. We should hold on to the value of the individual and the value of life at any cost.

7. Wouldn't a pro-euthanasia morality have a hard time dealing with mistakes and/or abuse of the law?

8. What about the danger that legal machinery initially designed to kill those who are a pain to themselves may some day engulf those who are pain to others?

Lawyer's Case for Euthanasia

1. What type of life would a baby have who was born a complete vegetable—the issue is quality of life not just being alive.

2. Special segregation and training involves heavy emotional and economic expense.

3. A carefully controlled system of euthanasia would eliminate the most helpless cases at once.

4. The quality of life of those around the incapacitated individual will be adversely affected if the individual is left to linger in pain.

5. There are those who are afflicted with incurable and painful diseases who want to die quickly. A law which tries to prevent such sufferers from achieving this quick death, and thereby forces other people who care for them to helplessly watch their pointless pain, is a cruel law! In such cases the sufferer may be reduced to an obscene image of a human being, a lump of suffering flesh eased only by intervals of drugged stupor.

6. There should be a concern for human dignity, an unwillingness to let pain disintegrate a person.

7. Suffering is evil. If it were not, why then do we expend so much energy in trying to relieve it?

8. The goal of the Euthanasia Society, "would permit an adult person of sound mind, whose life is ending with much suffering, to choose between an easy death and a hard one, and to obtain medical aid in implementing that choice."

EVANGELISM The Lifesaving Station

The following short parable is a great discussion starter on the subject of the church and the world. Either read it aloud or print it and hand it to your group.

Questions for discussion:

1. When was the Lifesaving Station most effective?

2. Where did the Lifesaving Station go wrong?

3. How is the church like a Lifesaving Station? What is the purpose of the church?

4. Is growth always good or desirable? Why? Why not?

5. Is growth inevitable if needs are being met?

6. If you don't like the church as it is now, what alternatives do you have?

7. What should the church do with all its money?

8. How can the problems that the Lifesaving Station experienced be avoided in the church? What should the Lifesaving Station have done?

9. Should Christians be part of a church? Why? Why not?

10. What are your church's good points? Bad points?

11. If you could write a moral that would be added to the end of The Lifesaving Station, what would it be?

The Lifesaving Station

On a dangerous sea coast where shipwrecks often occur, there was once a crude little lifesaving station. The building was just a hut, and there was only one boat, but the few devoted members kept a constant watch over the sea, and with no thought for themselves went out day and night tirelessly searching for the lost. Some of those who were saved, and various others in the surrounding area, wanted to become associated with the station and give of their time, money, and effort for the support of the work. New boats were bought and new crews trained. The little lifesaving station grew.

Some of the members of the lifesaving station were unhappy that the building was so crude and poorly equipped. They felt that a more comfortable place should be provided as the first refuge of those saved from the sea. They replaced the emergency cots with beds and put better furniture in the enlarged building.

The newly decorated and exquisitely furnished lifesaving station became a popular gathering place for its members, a sort of clubhouse. Fewer members were now interested in going to sea on lifesaving missions, so they hired lifeboat crews to do this work. The lifesaving motif still prevailed in the club's decoration, however, and there was a liturgical lifeboat in the room where the club initiations were held.

About this time a large ship was wrecked off the coast, and the hired crews brought in the boat loads of cold, wet, and half-drowned people. They were dirty and sick, and some of them had black skin and some had yellow skin. They dripped on the rug and water-stained the furniture in the beautiful new club. So the property committee immediately had a shower house build outside the club where victims of shipwreck could be cleaned up before coming inside.

At the next meeting, there was a split in the club membership. Most of the members wanted to stop the club's lifesaving activities as being unpleasant and a hindrance to the normal social life of the club. Some members insisted upon lifesaving as their primary purpose and pointed out that they were still called a lifesaving station. But they were finally voted down and told that if they wanted to save the lives of all the various kinds of people who were shipwrecked in those waters, they could begin their own lifesaving station down the coast. They did.

As the years went by, the new station experienced the same changes that had occurred in the old. It evolved into a club, and yet another lifesaving station was founded. History continued to repeat itself, and if you visit that sea coast today, you will find a number of exclusive clubs along that shore. Shipwrecks are frequent in those waters, but most of the people drown. ◇

Perfect Pair

FAMILY

For a good discussion on the family, and as a way to discover kids' values, try this. Divide into groups of five kids that are to create a description of the world's most perfect couple, that is, the man and woman best suited to create the ideal home and happy family. Things to consider:

1. The couple themselves
   a. background
   b. age
   c. education
   d. religious affiliation
   e. race
   f. political affiliation

2. Their lifestyle
   a. jobs (employment)
   b. hobbies
   c. sex life
   d. leisure time
   e. entertainment
   f. habits
   g. friends and associations

3. Their possessions
   a. money
   b. furniture
   c. house and neighborhood
   d. books, magazines
   e. appliances
   f. recreational needs
   g. auto(s)

4. Philosophy on child rearing
   a. discipline
   b. education
   c. manners
   d. dress
   e. independence

The items listed are only suggestions—the kids themselves already have ideas about what the perfect mom and dad would be like. After 30 minutes of small-group planning, ask each group to describe their perfect couple to the entire group. Record their ideas on the blackboard or on an overhead projector. Discuss the differences and similarities of each group's description, and ask why certain characteristics were selected. Ask them what description God gives of his perfect family. What matters and what doesn't? Also talk about the how the members in each small group interacted with each other—areas of agreement, differences of opinion, prejudices, etc.

Bug Me's

Here's a conversation catalyst for a youth-parent night to show it's often the little things we do that bug others in our family and that little irritations can lead to major problems.

Pass out copies of the "Bug Me" sheet shown on the next page for both kids and parents fill out. Collect and review them quickly to find out the most common responses for each question.

Next, divide into small groups and assign each one a different "Bug Me." One group, for example, might be given the most common answer to the first question on the list—"People taking too long in the bathroom in the mornings." That group discusses the following three questions about the "Bug Me" they received: 1) Is this a legitimate "Bug Me"? 2) What is the underlying problem and attitude causing this "Bug Me"? 3) What advice would the group give for solving the problem?

Finally, have each group share its answers with the others. Lead the group to recognize the pattern in the answers: The root problems behind most family "Bug Me's" are selfishness and thoughtlessness.

"Bug Me's"

1. What bugs you most at your house before school and work in the mornings?

2. What bugs you most at the family dinner table?

3. What bugs you most about your family on Sundays?

4. What bugs you most on family vacations?

5. What bugs you most about how parents communicate with their kids? (Youth answer only.)

6. What bugs you most about how kids communicate with their parents? (Parents answer only.)

7. What bugs you most about your family when it comes to household chores?

8. What bugs you most about your family when your friends are around you and your family?

9. What bugs you most during the times of deep family discussion (fights)?

10. What bugs you most about how your parents try to relate to or understand you kids? (Kids answer only.)

11. What bugs you most about how your kids try to relate to or understand you parents? (Parents answer only.)

12. What bugs you most at your house just around bedtime? ◇

FANTASY The Window

Read or tell the following story to the group. Use the questions at the end of the story to start the kids talking about the issues the story raises.

The Window

There were once two men, Mr. Wilson and Mr. Thompson, both seriously ill in the same room of a great hospital. Quite a small room, it was just large enough for the pair of them. It contained two beds, two bedside lockers, a door opening to the hall, and one window looking out on the world.

Mr. Wilson, as part of his treatment, was allowed to sit up in bed for an hour in the afternoon (something about draining the fluid from his lungs). His bed was next to the window. But Mr. Thompson had to spend all of his time flat on his back. Both of them had to be kept quiet and still, which was the reason they were in the small room by themselves. They were grateful for the peace and privacy, though. None of the bustle and clatter and prying eyes of the general ward for them. Of course, one of the disadvantages of their condition was that they weren't allowed to do much: no reading, no radio, certainly no television. They just had to keep quiet and still, just the two of them.

Well, they used to talk for hours and hours. About their wives, their children, their homes, their jobs, their hobbies, their childhoods, what they did during the war, where they'd been on vacations, all that sort of thing. Every afternoon when Mr. Wilson,

the man by the window, was propped up for his hour, he would pass the time by describing what he could see outside. And Mr. Thompson began to live for those hours.

The window apparently overlooked a park with a lake dotted with ducks and swans, where children tossed bread to the birds and sailed model boats, and young lovers walked hand in hand beneath the trees. And there were flowers and stretches of grass, games of softball, people taking their ease in the sunshine, and right at the back, behind the fringe of trees, was a fine view of the city skyline. Mr. Thompson would listen to all of this, enjoying every minute. He heard how a child nearly fell into the lake, how beautiful girls glided through the park in their summer dresses, how the baseball team made a home run, how a boy taught his puppy to chase a stick. Mr. Thompson felt he could almost see what was happening outside.

Then one fine afternoon when there was some sort of a parade, the thought struck him: Why should Wilson, next to the window, have all the pleasure of seeing what was going on? Why shouldn't he get the chance? He felt ashamed and tried not to think like that, but the more he tried the worse he wanted a change. He would do

anything! In a few days, he had turned sour. He should be by the window. He brooded. He couldn't sleep and grew even more seriously ill, mystifying the doctors.

One night as he stared at the ceiling, Mr. Wilson suddenly woke up coughing and choking, the fluid congesting his lungs. His hands groped for the call button that would bring the night nurse running. Mr. Thompson watched without moving. The coughing racked the darkness. Over and over he gagged and choked struggling to breathe. Then suddenly the noise stopped. There wasn't even the sound of breathing. Mr. Thompson continued to stare at the ceiling.

In the morning the day nurse came in with water for their baths and found Mr. Wilson dead. They took his body away quietly with no fuss.

As soon as it seemed decent, Mr. Thompson asked if he could be moved to the bed next to the window. So they moved him, tucked him in, made him quite comfortable, and left him alone to be quiet and still. The minute they'd gone, he propped himself up on one elbow, painfully and laboriously, and strained as he looked out the window.

It faced a blank wall. ◇

1. What was your initial reaction to the story? Were you shocked? Surprised? Angry?

2. From the story, describe Mr. Wilson. What kind of man does he appear to be? Do you like or dislike him? Why?

3. Describe Mr. Thompson? What kind of person is he? Do you like or dislike him? Why?

4. Why did Mr. Wilson do what he did? What do you think his motives were?

5. Would you describe Mr. Wilson's stories of what was happening outside the window as (a) lying? (b) products of a creative imagination? (c) evidence of his unselfish concern for Mr. Thompson? (d) cruel and done to make Mr. Thompson envious? (e) other.

6. Did Mr. Wilson do anything wrong?

7. Why did Mr. Thompson's mood change from enjoyment and appreciation to resentment? Was his resentment justified? Why or why not?

8. Did Mr. Thompson murder Mr. Wilson?

9. Who was guilty of the more serious wrong? Mr. Wilson or Mr. Thompson?

10. Who was most responsible for Mr. Wilson's death? Why?

11. Would both men have been better off without Mr. Wilson's descriptions of the view outside the window?

12. If you had been Mr. Thompson, how would you have felt when you finally looked out the window? (a) disappointed? (b) angry? (c) guilty? (d) grieved? (e) grateful? (f) puzzled? (g) shocked?

13. Is it a sin to fantasize?

14. Is it a sin to hide the truth or to exaggerate when it doesn't hurt anyone?

15. Where does one draw the line in the areas of fantasy and imagination?

FEAR Rotating Fear

This activity directs kids in evaluating the place fear should have in a person's life. Set up eight discussion centers around the room (fewer if your group is small). Write the statements below on 3 x 5 cards—one per card—and place one card at each center. Beside the statement card stack eight blank cards.

Divide the young people into eight small groups that will move from one center to another every five minutes. At each discussion center the group will talk about one of the eight statements (each center has a different statement), decide to agree or disagree with the statement, and record its decision.

Begin with one small group in each discussion center. When the leader blows a whistle or claps her hands, each group reads the statement at its center and then discusses the validity of the statement for five minutes. When the leader says "Vote" the groups must stop discussing, vote to agree or disagree with their statement, and record their vote on a blank card. When the leader claps again, each group rotates to the next center and repeats the procedure.

After each group has been through all eight areas, bring them together as a large group to tally the votes on each statement and share the findings. Discuss each statement further.

 # 1: You're riding on Space Mountain at Disney World. You find yourself screaming at the top of your lungs—in real fear. This fear is stupid. You should try your best to ignore it or repress it.

 # 2: You've watched horror movies about people being possessed by the devil. Demonic possession scares you. It sounds horrible and frightening. Actually, you shouldn't be afraid.

 # 3: You've just been caught skipping class. You face a chance of being suspended. You're scared. You ought to be.

 # 4: You've just returned from a tent revival meeting. The preacher talked about Hell and its horrors. The talk scared you. You don't want to go to Hell. You shouldn't be afraid.

 # 5: "There is no fear in love: but perfect love casts out fear, because fear involves punishment. And the one who fears is not perfected in love." 1 John 4:18

 # 6: You just read about an ax murderer. Later you're walking down a dark street, and you remember what you just read. You begin to wonder if the murderer is nearby. You begin to feel terribly afraid. This fear is childish. You should try to ignore or repress your fear.

 # 7: "The Lord is my light and my salvation: whom shall I fear?" Psalm 27:1. According to this, Christians should fear nothing.

 # 8: Fear is good.

Who Would You Choose?

Show your young people how quickly we form opinions about people based on what they look like. Hang up 20 or so photos of people of all kinds—old, young, Hispanic, Asian, white, black, attractive, ugly, fat, slim, wealthy, poor. Give everyone 15 minutes to study the photos.

Next, in groups of four or five, let the kids discuss these questions, making their choices from among the people in the photographs:

1. Which five people would you want to travel with for one year?

2. Is there any one person you would not want anything to do with? Why?

3. Who, if anyone, would you be willing to marry?

4. Who, if anyone, would you choose to be your best friend? Why?

5. Which person of the opposite sex do you think you could really like? Why?

6. If only five of those photographed and yourself were allowed to live while everyone else would be executed, which five would stay with you? Why?

7. What traits, other than how people look, would you use to answer the above questions?

FRIENDSHIP — Best Friends

Here's a case study dealing with friendship, forgiveness, cheating, priorities, and more.

Print up for everyone or read to them the following situation, and invite them to respond to the questions that follow.

Best Friends

Jack, a Christian, hadn't had time to do his homework the night before. There was a special speaker at his church, and Jack was attending and learning a lot. His best friend Bill, also a Christian, was enjoying the speaker, too, but he had done his homework in the afternoon. He didn't have a job, as Jack did.

So Jack asked Bill if he could copy his homework this morning. Just this once. Bill agreed. After all, he and Jack were best friends.

The next day as they picked up their homework papers at the end of the period, each had a note attached—"See me at the end of class." When they went up afterward, the teacher said, "It looks like you two copied off each other."

Wanting to be honest, Bill confessed—yes, they had copied off each other. The teacher then told them that they'd both receive F's for the assignment and that notes would be mailed home to inform their parents.

Jack was furious. Out in the hallway he let Bill know how angry he was—that their friendship was over. To this day neither has tried to renew the friendship. ◇

Follow up with a discussion and Bible study on these passages:

Colossians 3:12-14—Ask, "What is to be the measure of our forgiveness? How much are we to forgive?"

Matthew 6:14-15—Ask, "What will be the measure of God's forgiveness? How much will he forgive?"

Matthew 18:21-35—Ask, "What are the disciples learning?"

Questions for discussion:

Where did Jack go wrong? What did he do that he shouldn't have done?

1. Went to church to hear the speaker
2. Got a job
3. Asked to copy Bill's homework
4. Remained silent in front of the teacher
5. Became angry
6. Broke off the friendship
7. Never forgave Bill
8. Other

Where did Bill go wrong? What did he do that he shouldn't have done?

1. Went to church to hear the speaker
2. Did his homework
3. Let Jack copy his homework
4. Wanted to be honest
5. Confessed
6. Never forgave Jack
7. Other

Such Good Friends

Friendships are of primary importance to most young people. To help kids think through friendship, ask them to answer each of the following questions on their own before discussing them together with the group.

1. What is friendship?
   How do you define it?

2. Why do we need friends?

3. Describe the perfect friendship.

4. Describe a lousy friendship.

5. Name some of the qualities of a successful friendship that the following verses suggest:
   - 1 Samuel 18:1; 19:1-7
   - Job 2:11-13
   - Proverbs 17:17
   - Proverbs 27:5-6
   - Ecclesiastes 4:9-11
   - Mark 2:1-5
   - John 11:33-36

6. In what ways is God a very special friend? Read the following verses for ideas:
   - John 15:13
   - Romans 8:38-39
   - Hebrews 13:5-8
   - 1 Peter 5:7

7. Fill out this card for your three closest friends.

Friend's name _____

Why he or she is my friend _____
_____

What my friend contributes to our friendship _____
_____

What I contribute to our friendship _____
_____

How our friendship could improve
1. _____
2. _____
3. _____

FUTURE   Future World

Use this activity and discussion to alert youths to the effect today's activities and preparations have on their futures, and to how helpful the church can be in preparing them for the future.

First, divide the youths into small groups of three to four. Give each group three large sheets of paper and some markers. Then read the questions below one at a time, letting the kids suggest and discuss answers. Each group records its ideas on the large paper, then reports back to the entire group. Have a separate reporting time for each question.

Questions:

1. List some characteristics of the world as you think it will be in ten years.

2. List some characteristics of the kind of person who will best be able to deal with the world as it will exist ten years from now.

3. List five goals the church should adopt in order to prepare youths for living in the world of the future.

After all their answers have been presented and discussed, ask the kids what they are doing now to prepare themselves spiritually for the future. In responding to this last question, many will realize that the church is already attempting to prepare young people for the future, but they aren't taking advantage of all the opportunities offered. Youth workers may also discover some needs of their kids that are presently being overlooked.

Future Fantasy

Your kids can create a game that broadens their thinking about vocations and at the same time helps them get to know each others' vocational interests. On index cards each person writes three or four clues about the vocation he believes he might pursue in the next five or ten years, writing the name of the vocation at the top of the card. The vocations the kids choose should be serious, but their clues can be funny or serious. Ask all the kids to keep their vocations and clues a secret. Collect completed cards and shuffle them thoroughly.

Next, pass out blank sheets of paper. Ask the students to number the paper from one up to the number of youths at the meeting. While they're numbering their papers, number the cards you've collected. When all the papers and cards are ready, read aloud the clues on the first card, and ask everyone to write down a guess about who that person is. Remind them not to comment aloud on any of the cards or on their own responses. After you've read through all the clue cards, repeat any as needed for clarification.

Next, go through the cards again and ask the person who wrote each one to reveal herself. The results will be fun and surprising. Use the following questions, plus others of your own for discussion:

1. What do teenagers fear about the future?

2. What do you fear most about the future?

3. Read Matthew 6:25-34. Do you think God wants you to worry about the future? Why or why not?

4. What hope does God offer for your future?

Close with a prayer that your students' futures will be centered on God and his Word.

GOALS Life Goals

Hand out the following list of goals (adding any others that you want) and ask the kids to rate them as "Got to have it," "Would be nice," or "Not necessarily for me."

When they've finished, have the kids look up the following Scripture passages and determine what they have to say about setting goals: Psalm 27:4; 1 Kings 3:5-15; Philippians 3:7-10.

Next, have the kids list their top three goals, along with ways to achieve them.

1. A great family life without any hassles.
2. All the money I want.
3. Never to be sick or seriously injured.
4. To find a good-looking and fulfilling mate.
5. To do what I want when I want.
6. All the power the President has.
7. To be the best-looking person.
8. A great hunger for the Bible and prayer.
9. To be able to understand all things.
10. To eliminate all hunger and disease in the world.
11. To be always super-close to God.
12. Never to feel lonely or put down.
13. To know the future.
14. To be able to learn quickly and excel in all things.
15. To be filled with God's presence in the most dynamic way.
16. To know always that I'm in God's will.
17. To be the greatest athlete in the world.
18. To become a famous movie star.
19. To always have a lot of close friends who never let me down.

GOD Atheist Role Play

Sometimes it's a good idea to force kids to think through their reasons for believing in God (if they say they do) and to strengthen those beliefs. In addition, it is important to take kids a step further and help them see how their belief (or non-belief) in God makes a difference in the way they live.

Pair the kids off for a role play. One person takes the role of an atheist (a person who does not believe in God) and the other is a believer. One pair at a time, in front of the entire group, each student in a pair tries to convince the other one that his view is the correct one. Allow about three minutes per pair.

After everyone has taken a turn,

ask one of the youth sponsors to come before the entire group and take the position of the atheist. The group must try to convince him that he is wrong. Since the kids have had some practice in their individual role plays, they should be well equipped to the job.

For the next step give the kids pencils and paper to write down five things that would change in their lives if they knew for certain that there were no God. What difference would it make in the way they lived? Then ask them to write down five things that would probably change in their lives if they knew for a fact that God exists. In other words, would they live differently if, by appearing in the sky or talking out loud, God left absolutely no doubt that he

exists? How would they behave differently?

After the kids compare their own two lists and discuss the differences between both lists and the way they live right now, open further discussion with questions like the following:

1. On the basis of the arguments you've heard, do you believe in God or not? (Take a secret ballot vote if you want.)

2. Is it possible to "abstain" in a vote for or against the existence of God? In other words, can a person just not have an opinion? What are the consequences of such a position?

3. In what ways does how you believe affect the way you live right now?

God Is Like...

If someone asked you to describe God in terms they could relate to, what would you say? Traditionally, God has been called "the man upstairs," "a heavenly father," "a mighty judge," "a mother hen," and so on. Begin this exercise by

asking your students to recall phrases they've heard about what God is like.

The next step is to come up with some up-to-date descriptions of God, either individually or in small groups. Hand out pens and paper and instruct the kids to think of as many "God is like's" as they can in 10 minutes. Prime their pumps with examples like, "God is like Coke...he's the real thing" or "God is like Allstate...you're in good hands with him" or even "God is like a good student...he spreads his work over six days instead of pulling an all-nighter."

After 10 minutes, give each group a turn to read their comparisons while the other groups check for duplication on their own list. If two or more groups have the same comparisons, they must be scratched off all lists. The group with the most original comparisons left is the winner. Close by discussing the various images of God, and come to a consensus on the best four or five.

How God Works in My Life

Here's a good discussion starter on the topic of Providence. Look at Psalm 121 following the discussion.

Give everyone a sheet of paper to divide into three columns with the following headings: Primarily My Responsibility; Primarily God's Responsibility; Too Close to Call. Read the following list (or a similar list), pausing between each statement so the kids can place it in one of the columns. Let the kids compare answers and discuss their reasons for classifying the statements as they did.

1. Making the decision whether I marry or remain single.

2. Protecting me from drunken drivers.

3. My doing well when I perform a solo.

4. My decision to become a Christian.

5. Keeping me from illness.

6. Keeping me encouraged about the Christian life.

7. Choosing my vocation.

8. My understanding Scripture.

9. My understanding geometry.

10. Keeping me from doubt.

11. My financial condition.

12. My health.

Following this exercise, discuss how God may perform those functions that we feel he is responsible for.

Invent

Describe the situation below to groups of five to seven kids, allowing each group 20 minutes to finish its task. At the end of the allotted time, have the groups meet together and compare their responses.

Situation: You find yourself in a new civilization similar to our world now, but without God, religion, church, the Bible, or religious history. You are selected by your government to create a god that people want to worship. The character of your god should include qualities that you think not only attract people but at the same time explain things like natural disasters (flood, earthquake, etc.), sickness, suffering, and evil.

Questions to help you as you invent a god: What is the god's name, if any? Where does the god live? Is the god visible? If so, what does the god look like? Will your god make any demands on people? How do you worship the god? Any rewards or punishments? Is there more than one god? Does the god have any bad attributes? Just let your imagination run wild, and attempt to invent the perfect god that will attract the most people.

For discussion, compare the invented gods with the God of the Bible. The following questions could be included in the discussion:

1. Why is God so mysterious?

2. Why did God leave so many unanswered questions?

3. Why doesn't God make himself visible?

4. What things about God are the most difficult to believe?

5. What things would you change about God if you could?

GOSSIP The Disease of Diotrephes

Does your youth group have "Diotrephes Disease"? Is there a dictator or boss in the bunch who insists on having his own way? That type of personality can be disastrous in a youth group. Here's a Bible study and discussion guide that allows kids to evaluate their lives and attitudes to avoid this ancient form of "illness" described by the Apostle John:

"I wrote to the church, but Diotrephes, who loves to be first, will have nothing to do with us. So if I come, I will call attention to what he is doing, gossiping maliciously about us. Not satisfied with that, he refuses to welcome the brothers. He also stops those who want to do so and puts them out of the church" (3 John 9-10).

After reading together these words about Diotrephes, have the group consider the following six characteristics that can cause problems in the Christian community:

1. **He "loves to be first" (v. 9).** How does this desire usually show itself? Why do you think people want to be first? Is it possible for Christians to have this attitude? According to Mark 9:22-35, what did Jesus say to the disciples who had this problem? Instead of wanting to be first, what attitude should we have (Philippians 2:3-4)? How can we develop this attitude?

2. **He would "have nothing to do with us" (v. 9).** The "us" refers to John and his companions. Who was John? Why do you think Diotrephes would want to reject one of Jesus' apostles? Do we ever reject leaders in the church today? If so, how? What should our attitude be toward leaders in God's church (Hebrews 13:7,17)? How can we be more supportive of our leaders?

3. **He is "gossiping maliciously" (v. 10).** How would you define gossip? What happens in a group when gossip is a habit? What does God have to say about gossip in James 3:1-12 and Ephesians 4:25,29. How can we stop gossip in our group and begin practicing useful, helpful, encouraging speech.

4. **He "refuses to welcome the brothers" (v. 10).** Does this ever happen today? If so, how and why? Is there ever a time when we should separate ourselves from fellowship with certain believers? (Find out by reading Romans 16:17-18 and Titus 3:9-11.) Why is fellowship with other believers so important? What can

we do to improve our fellowship? What can we do to make new believers welcome?

5. **He "stops those who want to do so" (v. 10).** There were those who wanted to welcome John and the others, which obviously is the right thing to do. Do Christians ever keep fellow Christians from doing the right things? If so, how? What keeps us from doing what we know is right? What does God say in James 4:17 about knowing the right thing and not doing it? How can we develop a willingness to do what is right every time? How can we encourage one another to do what is right?

6. **He "puts them out of the church" (v.10).** Read 1 Corinthians 5:1-5 and Matthew 18:15-17 to discover when and why church discipline should be practiced by the local church. If it's practiced correctly, how does it help a church? Can church discipline ever harm a church? If so, how? What can we do to insure that correction of erring members is done in the right way for the right reason to accomplish the right results? How can our youth group practice this right kind of discipline?

With these insights in mind, every youth group member should ask, "Am I ever a Diotrephes?" "Is there another Diotrephes in our group that I could help in some way?" Then consider together whether your youth group as a whole suffers from the Diotrephes disease. If so, how can you be cured? How do visitors or new members see your youth group? What can be done to make your youth group more attractive and encouraging?

Decisions

Kids have ten minutes to decide which of the following things they consider to be the most harmful and to order the list using a number 1 beside the one they think is the most harmful, number 2 beside the second most harmful, etc. Afterward, discuss the results. Define harmful as it relates to all areas of life.

HARMFUL ACTIONS

____ Getting drunk
____ Moderate drinking (alcohol)
____ Lack of exercise
____ Cigarette smoking
____ Guilt feelings
____ Poor eating habits (types of food, how eaten, etc.)
____ Marijuana
____ Drugs (amphetamines, LSD, etc.)
____ Overwork
____ Lack of medical attention when necessary
____ Premarital sex
____ Nervous anxiety and tension
____ Fatigue, caused by never getting enough sleep

____ Overeating
____ Watching television
____ Reading pornography
____ Other:
____ Other:

Questions:

■ Why did you rank the items the way you did?

■ What criteria did you use to decide which item was more harmful then the others?

■ How would your parents rank the items?

■ How would God rank them?

HELPING PEOPLE

Saying the Right Thing

It is one thing to know we need to help people; it's quite another to know how to do it. Here is an exercise to help young people discuss practical options when helping someone.

The following situations give different options for a response to a specific problem. Discuss the pros and cons of each response and add whatever other responses you might think are appropriate. There are no right answers, but you should be able to discover that certain responses are more appropriate than others.

A woman is dying of cancer. She is not active in a church, but does attend worship services. She has three teenage children. You have been visiting her in the hospital. She has been telling you about her oldest son, who's been in some trouble. You have prayed with and for her and are excusing yourself to leave. She begins crying. What do you say/do now? Why?

1. Is there anything you'd like to share with me?

2. I see you have some deep feelings. What are you crying about?

3. It's really difficult being in the hospital when you're concerned about your children, isn't it?

4. Listen, I'll go see your son and try to help.

5. I've got a great book that really will help you with the problem.

6. I'm sorry...Good-bye.

7. I'll send the pastor over.

8. Don't cry...everything will be all right.

9. Listen, don't worry, God will work it all out.

You have a good friend (your age) whose father suddenly died. After missing several days of school, your friend just returned to classes. You see him for the first time since his dad's death. What do you say/do?

1. I hear your father just died. Gee, that's too bad.

2. Boy, I know just how you feel.

3. I'm really sorry about your dad. I don't know what I'd do if my dad died.

4. I'm sorry about your dad, but at least he's in heaven.

5. Hey, how you doin'? Good to see you.

6. Boy, you and your dad were really close, weren't you? It must be tough.

7. What's happening, man? Hey listen, a bunch of us are getting together for a big party this weekend, what are the chances of you coming?

Your brother (or sister) has just had a fight with your mom and dad. It seems that your parents forgot to tell him that they had something planned for Saturday so he will have to cancel his plans for Saturday. Your brother stomps angrily back to his room and is grumbling about how unfair the situation is. What do you say/do?

1. Boy, did you get the shaft!

2. What are you complaining about, you got to go out last weekend!

3. Let's forget to tell Mom and Dad about the next thing we've got planned.

4. What happened?

5. Hey, look, we'll figure out something to do here at home.

6. I think Mom and Dad are right.

7. Quit acting like a baby!

You might try role playing each of these situations.

HUNGER — Don't Talk with Your Mouth Full

In most of our affluent churches, the young people need to evaluate their attitudes toward food and fasting. Equip them for the discussion by studying biblical fasts to determine the relevance or need for fasting today. Below are a few quotes, references, and discussion questions that can stimulate interest in the topic.

Quotes:

1. "Food is not the most basic essential in life. The greatest bodily need is air. The second is not food, but water. Third is not food, but sleep! Food comes fourth. But thousands of Christians make food number one. Too much food clogs the system. To overeat is a sin of waste and a sin against the body, shortening the physical life and dulling the spiritual. If you are not its master, you are its slave!" Winkie Pratney

2. "The appetite for food is perhaps more frequently than any other the cause for backsliding and powerlessness in the church today. God's command is 'whether you eat or drink or whatsoever you do, do all to the glory of God.' Christians forget this and eat and drink to please themselves. They consult their appetites instead of the laws of life and health. More persons are snared by their tables than the church is aware of. A great many people who avoid alcohol altogether will drink tea and coffee that in both quality and quantity violate every law of life and health. Show me a gluttonous professor, and I will show you a backslider." Charles Finney

3. "It is important for us to distinguish between a desire or appetite for food and a hunger for food. It is doubtful whether the average individual, reared in our well-fed Western civilization, knows much of genuine hunger. The sensation of emptiness or weakness, gnawing in the pit of the stomach and other symptoms experienced at the outset of a fast are seldom real hunger. They are a craving for food resulting from the habit of feeding ourselves three times a day without intermission for 365 days a year." Arthur Wallis

Questions for discussion:

1. How do you react to Finney's statement? Why?

2. What do you think Finney meant when he used the phrase "the appetite for food"?

3. How could Finney link the idea of "powerlessness in the church" with the "appetite for food"? Do you think it is valid?

4. How is it possible to eat to the glory of God?

5. How much gluttony does it take to make one gluttonous?

6. What is your definition of fasting?

7. Is fasting a valid form of worship for people today? Why?

Image of Christ   JESUS

Here's a short discussion starter on the person of Jesus Christ. Divide the group into small groups that will each discuss one of the Scripture references given below. Then have each group match the scriptural "image of Christ" to their selection. Ask one person from each group to explain the image her group discovered in their reading.

Scripture:
1. Philippians 2:5-11
2. Matthew 25:34-40
3. Isaiah 42:1-9
4. John 10:11-16
5. John 6:44-51
6. Luke 4:38-41
7. Matthew 16:13-20

Image:
1. Lord and servant
2. Kind and friend
3. Suffering servant
4. Shepherd
5. Teacher and bringer of life
6. Compassionate
7. Peter's confession

Jesus' Report Card

Rate the following statements on a scale of one to five according to whether or not you agree with them. Five means strongly agree, three is neutral, and one is strongly disagree.

____ a. Jesus Christ lived about 2000 years ago, and what he did and said has no meaning for me today.

____ b. When Jesus lived, he was a great teacher, but the things he taught are not relevant today.

____ c. Most people do not read the Gospels because they are afraid that their interpretations might differ from that of their church or be incorrect.

____ d. If the gospel or Jesus were on TV as a regular series, most people would watch it.

____ e. The Gospels are more meaningful when they given a modern translation.

____ f. Jesus asked too much of his followers.

____ g. Jesus had a normal relationship with his family.

____ h. Jesus performed miracles to prove how great he was.

____ i. Jesus had to be baptized.

____ j. Jesus probably didn't do many of the things the Gospels say that he did. The Gospels are just the writers' stories and imaginations.

Is there anything you think Jesus should have done to make his message more acceptable to people?

Is there anything in the Gospel that you cannot accept? What?

Letter to Amos

JUSTICE

Get the kids talking about the Old Testament book of Amos by reading together this "open letter" to Amos and discussing the arguments presented. Some suggested questions for discussion follow.

Questions for discussion:

1. Evaluate the merchant's arguments in light of justice. At what points does the businessman convince or fail to convince you?

2. Suppose this letter were written today—how would you react? Where do the rights of the individual stop? Can justice be administered without striking a balance between individual rights and rights of the community?

3. What about Justice, Just Us, or Just U.S.?

Dear Mr. Amos,

Your intemperate criticisms of the merchants of Bethel show that you have little understanding of the operations of a modern business economy. You appear to not understand that a businessman is entitled to a profit. A cobbler sells shoes to make money—as much as he can. A banker lends money to get a return on his loan. These are not charitable enterprises. Without profits, a tradesman cannot stay in business.

Your slanders also reveal a lack of appreciation for the many contributions made to our land by the business community. Visitors to Israel are greatly impressed by the progress made in the past few decades. The beautiful public buildings and private homes are proud monuments. Increasing contacts with foreign lands add to the cultural opportunities open to our citizens. Our military strength makes us the envy of peoples already swallowed up by their enemies.

Despite the great gains during Jereboam II's reign, there is some poverty. That we admit. But is it just to blame us for the inability of some people to compete? You say that the peasants were cheated out of their lands. Not so! They sold their property. Or in some cases it was sold for back taxes. Some peasants put up their land as collateral on a loan, then failed to meet the payments. No one was cheated. The transactions to which you refer were entirely legal. Had you taken the trouble to investigate the facts, your conclusions would have been more accurate.

The real reason for poverty is lack of initiative. People who get ahead in this world work hard, take risks, overcome obstacles. Dedication and determination are the keys to success. Opportunities don't knock; they are created by imagination and industry.

Our success can be an inspiration to the poor. If we can make it, they can too. With the growth of business, Israel grows. More jobs, better pay, and increased opportunity for everyone. The old saying contains more than a germ of truth; What's good for General Chariots is good for the country.

Yours for Israel, _____

LISTENING

Lesson on Listening

It can often come as a shock when we learn how much of our energy in conversations is used for "ego-speaking" and self-expression rather than for listening. The following exercise is designed to help your kids become aware of how easy it is to not listen to the messages of others.

To begin, prepare four cards as follows:

Your Favorites:
1. What do you like most about school?
2. What is your favorite time of year?
3. What is your favorite Bible verse?

The Pits:
1. What bugs you the most about school?
2. What is your least favorite vegetable?
3. When were you last bummed out?

Exposing Weaknesses:
1. What is your greatest personality weakness?
2. What is your most annoying habit?
3. What is your greatest spiritual weakness?

Revealing Strengths:
1. What is your most positive personality trait?
2. What is your greatest skill?
3. What is your best spiritual strength?

Divide everyone into groups no larger than five people. Each group should be given one of the four cards to discuss. Each group member briefly tells her answers to the questions on the card to the others in the small group. After about five minutes the groups exchange cards so that they have a new set of questions. As before, the group members take turns answering them.

When all the groups have discussed all four categories, ask each person to list on a sheet of paper every fact he can remember from the answers given in the small group. Of course, those with better memories are at a slight advantage, but those who really tuned in and listened to others in their group (rather than concentrating on their own responses) will be able to recall the most. For some helpful verses, take a look at Proverbs 18:2,13; 22:17, and Ecclesiastes 3:7.

How Love Is Expressed

This discussion starter explores the ways that Christian love is expressed in different relationships. The method is role play and discussion.

Divide into four groups and assign each group a situation to role play. The groups are specifically instructed to express Christian love in the situation they role play. Each group will present their role play and follow it up by asking the question, "How was Christian love expressed?" Everyone recalls the ways the actors expressed love and lists these as well other possible ways that were not acted out.

Analyze the list created. Discuss the different levels of love, possibly bringing up the biblical distinction between agape, eros, and phileo.

Here are four situations. Adjust the number of characters and their sexes to fit your group.

1. John and Mary return to Mary's home to tell her parents that they have become engaged. They have gone together for one and half years and are both in their 20s. John will graduate from college in May.
Characters: mother, father, John, Mary.

2. A black (use any ethnic group) family moved next door. Neighbors circulated a petition protesting the supposed lowering of property values, and you were one of the few home owners not to sign. You have observed another neighbor snub the new family. You wish to make them welcome. You and your son knock on the door, and the black man and his son answer.
Characters: a black father and son, a white father and son.

3. A pastor takes three church youths to visit an elderly lady. She lives alone in a rundown house.
Characters: pastor, three youths, the old lady.

4. You and your wife are Christians. An old atheist college roommate is visiting you. Conversation turns to religion, and the friend expresses hostility toward the church. He says, "The church is full of hypocrites."
Characters: a man and his wife, an atheist friend.

This Little Bite of Mine

This discussion starter helps your group talk about love. Read the story below to your group:

I heard a story about a man who was bitten by a dog. When the health officer tested the dog, sure enough, it was rabid. As soon as the victim heard this, he grabbed a pad of paper and a pen and began writing as fast as he could.

"Hey, we can give you a serum, you know. You don't have to write out your will," said the health officer.

"Oh, I'm not writing my will," cried the bitten man. "I'm making a list of all the people I want to bite."

After reading the story, give your young people these instructions:

1. Put yourself in the man's place. Pretend that you have been bitten by a rabid dog, and make a list of five people you want to bite. Include a one- or two-word note by each name to remind you why you want to bite them. Leave an inch or so of space below each name.

2. Now turn this around. Pretend that you are afflicted by the infectious disease of love. List five people you would like to bite now. Make a note to remind you why and leave an inch below each name.

3. Now discuss what happened. Are any of the people on both lists? Why? Can you feel hate for someone and still love them? Is it possible to consciously love someone? In other words, if you calculate loving someone, is that love? If you have to tell someone you love them, do you really love them?

MARRIAGE To Marry or Not To Marry

The following questionnaire is a good discussion starter on the subject of marriage. Print it up and give the group enough time to think through their answers. Then discuss each question, trying to come up with a group consensus. Encourage everybody to give answers that honestly reflect their personal opinions, rather than answering them the way the church, or their parents, or tradition would want them to answer.

1. I think everyone should get married (put an "x" on the continuum).

DEFINITELY   DEFINITELY
   YES   NO
_____

2. If a person decides to marry, I think the best age for marriage would be: (check the age)

Girls

☐ 16   ☐ 20   ☐ 24   ☐ 28
☐ 17   ☐ 21   ☐ 25   ☐ 29
☐ 18   ☐ 22   ☐ 26   ☐ 30
☐ 19   ☐ 23   ☐ 27   ☐ Over 30

Boys

☐ 16   ☐ 20   ☐ 24   ☐ 28
☐ 17   ☐ 21   ☐ 25   ☐ 29
☐ 18   ☐ 22   ☐ 26   ☐ 30
☐ 19   ☐ 23   ☐ 27   ☐ Over 30

3. When you are married, are you considered an adult regardless of age? (check one) ☐ YES ☐ NO

4. God has made one special person in the world for you to marry. (Put an "x" on the continuum)

STRONGLY   STRONGLY
 AGREE   DISAGREE
_____

5. Marriage is: (order these from 1 to 5 according to which phrase you think is the most important description of marriage)

____ A legal statement
____ A social custom
____ God ordained
____ A religious ceremony
____ A parent pleaser
____ Other:_____

6. Most people get married because: (rank these from 1 to 5)

____ They have to
____ They want to have kids
____ They love each other
____ Tax benefits
____ Sex
____ Other:_____

7. Our concept of marriage is most influenced by: (pick top three)

____ Friends   ____ Television
____ Movies   ____ Other Adults
____ Parents   ____ Church
____ Books   ____ Celebrities
____ Tradition
____ Other:_____

8. What are the top priorities in marriage: (rank from 1 to 10)

____ Children
____ Sex
____ Communication
____ Mutual Trust/Confidence in the other person
____ Religion/Faith
____ Mutual interests
____ Finances/Security
____ In-law relationships
____ Faithfulness
____ Romantic Love
____ Other:_____

9. Divorce is wrong: (choose the best answer or answers)

☐ Always (no exceptions)
☐ Except when adultery is involved
☐ Except when both are incompatible
☐ Except when you don't love each other any more
☐ Other: _____

10. Divorce is: (choose the best answer or answers)

☐ Better than living together when you hate each other
☐ A necessary evil
☐ A possibility for any one of us
☐ A cop out
☐ Never okay when children are involved
☐ Sin
☐ Other:_____

11. Living together (not married) is: (put an "x" on the continuum)

WRONG   OKAY
(ALWAYS)   (ALWAYS)
_____

12. Living together (not married) is: (choose best answer or answers)

☐ Better than the traditional custom of dating
☐ The best way to determine if marriage will last
☐ Is not the same as marriage
☐ Is more acceptable than marriage
☐ Is the best alternative to marriage
☐ None of the above
☐ Other:_____

Monitoring Your Morals

MORALS

The following are true-false questions to be answered individually and then discussed by the entire group. Explain that the answers given should be honest opinion, not answers that the church or youth director consider correct. Be prepared to work through each question thoroughly in the discussion period.

____ 1. Overeating is as wrong as smoking or drinking.

____ 2. While your father was walking home from work one night, a robber came from the shadows and demanded all his money. Your father gave his wallet to the robber. He looked in the wallet and asked, "Is this all the money you have?" Your father said, yes. The thief crept away satisfied, but your father had lied to the thief—he had $20 tucked away in his shirt pocket. This was wrong.

____ 3. To goof off on your job is as wrong as if you stole money from your boss.

____ 4. There are degrees of sin with God, and he won't punish us for the little ones.

____ 5. Killing a man is justified when a person is called by his government to defend his country.

____ 6. As Christians we are to obey all people who are in a position of authority over us. This means police officers, parents, teachers, youth directors, etc.

____ 7. You are late for church, so instead of driving at the 45 mph speed limit, you drive 50 mph. Because you are going to church this is not wrong.

____ 8. Going into your history final, you are just squeezing by with a C. Passing or failing this test could mean the difference between passing or failing this course. There are several questions you don't know answers to, so you look on your neighbor's paper—an A student— and copy from him. When you get your paper back, you find that you would have flunked without the correct answers from your neighbor's paper. Cheating was justified in this case.

____ 9. You are very much in love with your girlfriend and plan to marry her. On a date you get carried away, and she gets pregnant. Because you love her as you would your wife, the act was not wrong.

___ 10. There is a guy at school that really gets on your nerves. If there was ever a person that you hated, it would be this guy. The feeling you have for this guy is as wrong as if you killed him.

MOVIES   Movie Reviews

As cable television continues to increase in popularity and accessibility, young people watch more and more movies. In some communities there are as many as a dozen movie channels to choose from. In addition, more and more movies are being targeted directly at the adolescent audience.

In light of this trend, it's a good idea to view and discuss movies with your group. Use the work sheet below to guide your group in evaluating and discussing the movies they see.

Rent a videotape of a popular film to watch with your group. Let the kids know that movie makers use camera angles, lighting, background music, and special techniques on purpose to create an effect.

After viewing the movie, have the kids fill out the work sheet and discuss their answers. Other questions that would be good for discussion might include:

1. Is it dangerous to view a movie without thinking about what the film is really saying about the world?

How to Watch a Movie

Please view the movie with the rest of the group. While you are watching it, though, keep the following questions in mind—we will talk about them briefly after the flick. Remember, most movies are not made just for entertainment; there's a point to them. Let's see if we can discover it together.

1. Who do you think is the hero of this movie? Why?

2. Who is the villain or bad guy? Why?

3. Is there an evil in this movie? That is, what is the bad thing that could or does happen (for example, the hero dies or the universe is destroyed)?

How is that evil dealt with—what happens to it?

4. Summarize the basic story of the movie in one or two sentences.

5. What do you think the producer and director are trying to teach us with this movie?

6. Do you agree with what they're saying?

Thanks for answering these questions. I dare you to take a copy of this to the next movie you go see, or to fill one out after the next movie you watch on TV. Once you get the hang of thinking about what you watch, you'll enjoy movies a whole lot more!

2. Will this movie help me in my relationships (to God, my family, my friends)?

3. What does this movie have to say about biblical norms for living?

Sex in the Movies

Sexually explicit movie scenes mold the values of the teenagers who watch them. To generate discussion, ask some of the kids to tell about their favorite movie—or scene from a movie—and why they liked it. Then tackle the following questions in small-group discussion:

1. Do you think it's okay for actors and actresses to act in the nude or in sexually explicit scenes since they are only acting? Why or why not?

2. Why do you think current movies contain so much sexually explicit material? What is its purpose?

3. Do you believe that the movies present an accurate portrayal of sexual behavior or male/female relationships? Why or why not?

4. Do you think Christians should view sexually explicit films? Why or why not?

Would the age or maturity of the viewer change your answer?

5. What kinds of effects might viewing sexually explicit scenes have on you? On your relationships with others? On your relationship with God?

After the small groups come back together, ask a student to read aloud one or more of the following Scripture passages. Ask what insight, if any, they offer to the discussion of watching sexually explicit movies.

GET 'EM TALKING

Matthew 5:27-30
Ephesians 5:1-12
1 Thessalonians 4:1-8
Genesis 2:22-25; 3:1-12

In the large-group discussion that follows, point out some of the possible effects of viewing sexually explicit material including sexual arousal at inappropriate times, lust, guilt or shame, and a questioning of God's standards for sexual behavior. Encourage the kids to consider these and other possible effects when they're making decisions about film viewing.

MTV MTV!

Why not discuss the content and message of a few popular music videos with your youth group. Videotape a few selected hits and play them back for the group to watch together. Then discuss them using the work sheet below. Print additional sheets for the kids to fill out at home after watching some of their favorite music videos.

MTV!

We all know what an idiot is—a person who does things without thinking about them. When you call someone an idiot, it is an insult. A vidiot is almost the same thing. You are a vidiot if you watch music videos for any period of time without stopping to think about what they are saying. A vidiot lets other people influence her mind without even asking questions.

Watch the following videos and record your thoughts about them on this paper. Keep Philippians 4:8-9 in mind as you watch the video:

"Here is a last piece of advice. If you believe in goodness and if you value the approval of God, fix your minds on whatever is true and honorable and just and pure and lovely and praiseworthy. Model your conduct on what you have learned from me, on what I have told you and shown you, and you will find that the God of peace will be with you." (J.B. Phillips translation)

Name of song: _____

_____

Artist: _____

1. Do you like this video? Why or why not?
2. What did the visuals have to do with the song?
3. What was the song about?
4. What did the person singing the song want to happen? Is that a good thing to have happen? Why or why not?
5. As a Christian do you think that this video is healthy for someone to watch or listen to? Why or why not?
6. Does it fit the qualifications that Paul wrote about in Philippians? How?

Armageddon Bomber

Armageddon Bomber can be used with several groups in different rooms. Each group should include four people: pilot, bombardier, radio controller, and co-pilot. Give the following information to each group:

The year is 1999. You are the flight team of an advanced, ultra-modern U.S. bomber, and you are flying maneuvers over the Atlantic. You suddenly receive a highly classified message:

Emergency Alert: Code Red...U.S. has received nuclear attack by USSR. Casualties and destruction not known at this time. U.S. unable to retaliate...total destruction is imminent. You are carrying advanced nuclear warhead. Only hope. Your location pinpointed half way between U.S. and USSR. Your fuel at 50 percent. Maintain radio silence and proceed with operation Ranger Red. Deliver warhead.

The decision to fulfill the mission must be unanimous. If you decide not to fulfill the mission, your options are as follows:

1. You will change course and attempt to land in Greenland and hope the contamination has not reached you.

2. You will attempt to crash the plane in the target area rather than stay alive.

3. You will surrender to the enemy.

4. You will commit suicide and not drop the bomb.

5. You will simply keep flying and hope that you can get a clear picture of the situation and make up your mind at the last possible minute.

6. You will fly back to the U.S. to assess damage and hope that you can refuel somewhere.

After the time is up have each group share their decision and the reasons for it. Here are some possible questions:

1. What teachings of Jesus apply to this situation?

2. How much of your decision was influenced by your beliefs?

PARENTS How To Raise Your Parents

Here are some good questions for a discussion about parents. For best results, print them up and give one set of questions to each person. Give the kids time to answer all the questions individually. Then discuss them one at a time with the entire group.

POOR		AVERAGE		GREAT
1	2	3	4	5

1. How would you rate your relationship with your parent(s)?

2. What are some of the problems in your relationship with your parent(s)?

3. What are some of the good points of your relationship with your parent(s)?

4. What would help improve the relationship?

5. What do the following verses teach about relationships with parents?

Colossians 3:20
Proverbs 3:1-4
Exodus 20:3

6. Rate yourself in the following areas from 1 (almost never) to 5 (almost always).

____ a. I obey my parents in all things.

____ b. I am patient with my parent's weaknesses.

____ c. I apologize to my parents when I hurt them.

____ d. I trust God to change my parents if they are wrong.

____ e. I do more than my parents ask of me.

____ f. I try to see life fro m my parent's point of view.

____ g. I ask my parents for their advice.

____ h. I thank my parents for all they do for me.

____ i. I pray for my parents.

____ j. I show my parents I love them.

____ k. I tell my parents I love them.

____ l. I live the kind of life my parents can be proud of.

7. The area that I most need to improve is:

8. Check any of the following ideas you'd like to commit yourself to do in the next 48 hours:

____ Buy my mother flowers

____ Tell my parents I love them

____ Ask my parents to pray with me

____ Write a note of appreciation to my parents

____ Take my parents out to eat

____ Do some chores without being told

____ Ask my parent for some advice

____ Wash the car

____ Give my parents a hug or kiss

Parent Opinions

Give kids a "Question of the Week" to take home and ask their parents to answer. Here are questions to get you started:

■ What's the most important goal in your life?

■ If marijuana were legalized, would it still be wrong to smoke it?

■ One question I'd like to ask God is...

■ How do you stand on the abortion issue?

■ What's the greatest problem facing people your age?

■ How is being a teenager today different from when you were a teenager?

■ What's the hardest part of being a parent?

■ If you could change one thing about yourself, what would you change? Have the kids bring their parents' answers to the next meeting to discuss and compare with their own.

Parent/Teen Eye-Opener

This activity helps young people see that the struggle they may be having with their parents isn't all their parents' fault. It can be a real eye-opener for the kids and a peacemaker in the midst of family strife.

Give a 3 x 5 card to each person in your group. Then have them draw a line down the middle of the card and write "Mom" above one column and "Dad" above the other. Tell the kids that they

will be asked ten questions, and they are to answer them separately for their mothers and fathers. They must grade their parents on a scale of 1 to 10, with 1 being the lowest or worst possible grade and 10 the highest or best. Here are the questions:

1. Do your parents show you affection?

2. Do your parents listen to you?

3. Do your parents talk with you about

school work? Your interests? Your boy/girlfriend?

4. Do your parents trust you?

5. Do your parents respect you?

6. Do your parents initiate leisure activities that involve you (shopping, camping, tennis, walks)?

7. Do your parents treat your friends the way you want them to be treated?

8. Do your parents always have a settled opinion about things? (a "1" indicates they do, a "10" means they don't)

9. Do your parents respect your privacy?

10. Do your parents treat you the way you want to be treated?

After both parents have been graded on these items, discuss the kids' answers on a few random questions.

What usually follows is a discussion of all the things parents do wrong. But the kicker in this exercise is the next step. After the discussion, have the kids turn their cards over and again make two columns with the headings "Mom" and "Dad." But this time they are to grade themselves, using the same questions turned around. (For example: Do you show your mom affection? Your dad?) In this way they can think about their relationship to both their mothers and fathers. The young people will likely see that, in many cases, their attitudes toward their parents are very similar to their parents' attitudes towards them. Close the discussion by having the kids think of ways they can improve the relationship with their parents.

PATIENCE Patience Role Play

This idea works well with the topic of either patience or self-control. Guide the kids in an impromptu role playing of several scenarios from daily family life that would test any kid's (or parent's)

patience. Seeing family-life scenes from the parents' as well as the kids' perspectives helps make this exercise an effective reminder of the need to cultivate patience in daily life.

Here are suggestions for scenarios:

1. Your grandmother asks you to come over to help her set up the Christmas decorations. She ends up telling you exactly where to put every single light and strand of tinsel.

2. **Parent:** You have just come home from a long day at the office, and your son is glued to the television. You see that the dishwasher is not unloaded, which was something you asked him to do this morning.
Child: You have made your bed for the first time this summer, but you forgot to unload the dishwasher, which your mother asked you to do this morning.

3. Your aunt comes to visit for three weeks and stays in your room. One day you find her going through your drawers because, she says, she's interested in "finding out more about young people today."

4. You are the coach of an all-state team. The captain approaches you and says she can't come to preseason practice because she's going to church camp.

5. Your son has gone to the prom, promising to be home by 2:00 a.m. At 3:30 a.m. you suddenly wake up and discover he isn't home yet. He finally comes in at 4:00.

6. You're nice to the class geek for a day, and he (she) thinks you're in love with him (her).

7. You've got a great idea about the theme of the novel you're reading in English class, but the teacher says you're wrong.

After all the situations have been acted out and reacted to by the rest of the group, divide into small groups and discuss patience.

Questions for discussion:

1. What makes us feel frustrated? (feelings of helplessness, vulnerability, whatever)

2. How should Christians handle impatience?

3. Do you think God tests us? Why or why not?

4. When and why do you get impatient with God?

5. How can we become more patient?

6. How does the Holy Spirit change us in this and other areas?

PEACEMAKING Courtroom Drama

Vandals Attack Metropolitan School
600 lockers opened, contents strewn in hallways

Vandals struck the Metropolitan Intermediate School early Friday, breaking into 600 to 700 lockers and strewing books, binders, and clothing throughout the hallways.

County sheriff's deputies spent several hours at the school looking for clues to the identity of the culprit or culprits, sheriff's officials said. Late Friday afternoon, however, sheriff's deputies said they had no suspects in the case.

The students weren't allowed to see the damage at first, seventh-grader Lani Johnson said. But when they did see, they got angry, she said.

"Every hallway had piles of books on the ground. It looked like there had been a riot here," she said.

"The teachers are trying to keep everybody calm. But most of the kids are so mad...There was an awful lot of cussing going on here today."

There was a dance at the school the previous night, Principal Roy Stapleton said. There were no signs of vandalism or suspicious activi-ty when the custodian left the school grounds at 11:30 p.m. Thursday, Stapleton said.

When the morning custodian came on duty at 6:30 a.m. Friday, it was a different matter, he said.

Locks had been knocked off of somewhere between 600 and 700 lockers, he said. The contents of hundreds of lockers were thrown to the ground. Other lockers were jammed shut by repeated blows in an apparent attempt to break off their locks.

Although district officials still are investigating the extent of the damage, Stapleton said nothing of value appeared to be missing.

"It was vandalism. It wasn't burglary," he said.

When the seventh and eighth graders returned to the campus Friday morning, they were told to go to their first-period classes and were kept there, he said.

First-period teachers extended their usual one-hour lesson to two and a half hours, said one student teacher who asked not to be identi-fied. "It went pretty smoothly," she said. "We improvised a lot."

Meanwhile school officials, custodians, and parent volunteers cleaned up the mess, Stapleton said. The clothes were put in plastic garbage bags in the nurse's office. The books were stacked in the school library. Binders were piled in another room.

Surveying piles of bags on the floor, Stapleton said his staff and district officials would be sorting through the items over the weekend looking for clothing name tags and any names written inside books or binders so that they can be returned to their proper owners.

The Metropolitan School District, which normally charges a student for a lost or damaged book, would probably make exceptions for some of the students, he said.

By Friday afternoon, the school had returned to a normal routine, he said.

Try this courtroom drama for some stimulating discussion about issues such as justice and peacemaking on a personal scale. Begin by reading to the group the news article reproduced here, "Vandals Attack Metropolitan School." Then announce that your group will be enacting the legal case "Roger & Rip Locker vs. Mother District," based on the article.

Read aloud the following role descriptions and appoint someone to take each role.

Roger & Rip Locker: Two brothers attending the school are vandal **suspects** in the case. They are being sued for a half million dollars.

Dr. Locker: Roger and Rip's father. He wants to clear his name and medical practice by clearing his boys. He has $10,000 to work with.

Defense Attorney: Hired by Dr. Locker to defend Roger and Rip.

Oliver Do Ismyjob: Custodian on the late-night shift. Dr. Locker is his physician and friend of 20 years. Oliver saw Roger and Rip at the dance.

Lani Johnson: A student who was vandalized. She's angry and afraid that she and her friends will have to pay for their lost and damaged books.

Mrs. Johnson: Lani's mother, a parent volunteer who helped clean up the mess. She is protective of her daughter and has a close friend on the Herald newspaper staff—Allison Williams.

Allison Williams: She is an honest writer, but will do anything for the "right" story. What she writes in the papers can easily affect the lives of others.

Prosecuting Attorney: She wants to sue Roger and Rip Locker and their parents for a half million dollars to pay for all new lockers (600 were broken) and for damaged and lost books.

Roy Stapleton: School principal. He wants this kind of thing never to happen again. He is upset with the custodial staff and wonders why they couldn't have prevented the crime. He will charge students for the lost and damaged books if the district doesn't win the case. He knows Lani Johnson is a spoiled child who always get what she wants.

Bob Wegsteen: Math teacher who likes both Roger and Rip. They were the first ones to join his math club this year.

Janice Ames: The student teacher quoted in the article who had a run-in with Roger when she saw him cheat on a history test. She chaperoned at the dance

Thursday night and noticed Roger wandering through the halls several times during the evening.

Bonnie Bell: Rip's ex-girlfriend; she broke up with him at the dance. Her locker was never touched.

School Superintendent: He hired the prosecuting lawyer to prosecute Roger and Rip and wants these boys to be examples to all other vandals.

Judge: Listens and decides case outcome and verdict.

Jury Members: Must decide the case. Choose as many as you want, according to the size of your group.

Next, give everyone half an hour to prepare for the trial. The defense attorney should get with the defendants and witnesses to build their case. The school superintendent and prosecuting attorney should also interview witnesses to construct their case. The characters should not be allowed to talk to the judge or jurors while they make their "deals" prior to the trial.

As the characters are wheeling and dealing, set up the room to resemble a courtroom. When it's time for the trial to begin, have the characters take their places and follow this procedure:

1. The prosecution presents its case.

2. The defense presents its case.

3. The prosecutor calls on witnesses. These are first examined by the prosecution, then cross-examined by the defense, then examined again by the prosecution if desired.

4. The defense calls on witnesses. These are examined by the defense, cross-examined by the prosecution, and examined again by the defense if desired.

5. The prosecution makes its closing statement (no one else should talk).

6. The defense makes its closing statement (again, no one else should talk).

7. The judge and jurors are given up to ten minutes to decide the case.

After the trial, you can launch into a discussion of any one of a number of topics. One possibility is peacemaking. You would read Matthew 5:9 together and then ask the following questions:

1. What difference might it have made in the trial if each character had been a peacemaker? (Consider each character individually.)

2. What difference might it have made before the trial if those involved in the situation (principal, students, parents, teachers) had been peacemakers?

Peer Pressure Study

No youth group can afford to ignore the subject of peer pressure and conformity. The power that one's age group has to consciously or unconsciously force others to conform to the group's thinking and behavior can be a major obstacle in your kids' spiritual development. The following study is helpful as a means of opening up discussion on the topic. It also presents some valuable tools that your kids can use to battle peer pressure.

Two Biblical Examples

In the Old Testament we read how Daniel and his three friends were taken prisoners when the Babylonian army defeated Israel in 604 B.C. (Daniel 1). Daniel was probably about 16 years old at the time. He was taken from his country, his home, his school, and his parents and carried several hundred miles away to the Babylonian capital. He and his three friends were to be trained to serve the king.

They were suddenly faced with an intense test of their values. Would they continue to worship God or bow to the Babylonian idols? Would they break the Jewish dietary laws that they knew God had given them to keep them healthy and undefiled for his service? How would they react to the immoral practices of their captors?

They could easily have gone along with the crowd and compromised their values. But years before, they had

A Quiz

Take this Peer Pressure Survey to see how you react to peer pressure:

1. When faced with a decision to act or not to act like others my age are acting, I usually:

a. Flip a coin

b. Freak out and hide under my bed

c. Really think it over

d. Pray and ask God to show me what to do

e. Other:_____

2. I (often/sometimes/never) feel pressured to do something that others are doing in order to be accepted.

3. There is a right and a wrong choice for each decision I must make.
☐ Yes ☐ No

4. All peer pressure is bad.
☐ Yes ☐ No

5. There is peer pressure to act a certain way in our youth group.
☐ Yes ☐ No

6. The pressure I face most often is...

7. A Christian writer named Søren Kierkegaard once wrote, "There is a view of life which conceives that where the crowd is, there is also the truth. There is another view of life which conceives that wherever there is a crowd there is untruth."

Which view do you agree with?

8. In order of their importance to you, list five values or priorities in your life that you could use to guide you in making a decision:

1. _____

2. _____

3. _____

4. _____

5. _____

decided to put God's values above the values of people. Daniel and his three friends had already set their priorities; there was no further decision to make.

In the New Testament (John 7:1-7), Jesus' brothers encouraged him to visit the believers in Judea. No doubt the argument was persuasive. Jesus, however, was in touch with the larger plan and perfect will of God the Father. Nothing, not even his brothers' pleas, could veer him from that plan.

Making Decisions

Facing peer pressure comes down to one thing—what your priorities are. What values do you place the most importance on? Jesus tells us to "seek first the Kingdom of God and his righteousness" (Matthew 6:33). As Christians we should put God and his will for our lives first, above everything else. You can ask yourself three questions about a choice:

1. How does it affect me as an individual?

2. How will it affect others?

3. How will it affect the cause of Christ? You can apply three tests to each choice you face:

1. The test of secrecy. Would you feel different if someone else you knew was aware of what you were doing?

2. The test of individuality. Would you still do it even if all of your friends were not?

3. The test of prayer. Can you ask God to go with you and bless you in this?

And finally, there are three sources of spiritual guidance for you:

1. From within—your conscience and the Holy Spirit.

2. From without—your parents (they do know something), Christian friends, and church leaders.

3. From above—your relationship with Jesus Christ and your understanding of what the Bible has to say.

Dear Abby

Occasionally young people encounter situations in which they would like advice from a Christian perspective, but are embarrassed to bring their questions openly before their peers. This discussion starter sidesteps that problem.

Give everyone paper and pen to write in letter form questions they're wondering about and problems they need answers to. They can be family struggles, problems at school—any problems or questions that require Christian advice.

The letter should be addressed to "Dear Abby" (to give the feeling of appealing to some uninvolved source) and signed with an anonymous signature ("Concerned" or "Wants to Know").

Then collect the letters, read them to the group, and let the kids advise each other. This not only gives the group a chance to help, but they learn that others experience problems similar to their own.

Gospel According to Dear Abby

Select from assorted "Dear Abby" and "Ann Landers" columns letters that reflect problems relevant to your youth group. Then read one of the letters to your group without the columnist's reply. (Note: If your group is large, give one letter to each small group.) Lead the kids to discuss how they think Jesus would have answered the letter. After sufficient discussion, read the columnist's reply and compare her answer with Jesus' hypothetical answer.

Discuss the differences, if any.

Read as many letters as time allows, skipping the ones that don't generate any interest.

Another twist to this would be to have each individual write a response to the Dear Abby letter, and then let the kids compare answers. Using each person's letter as a resource, have the group compile a group letter combining the best elements of each individual letter.

Problem Letter

Most youth leaders who have any rapport at all with kids receive numerous requests for help. These requests are a valuable resource for intragroup, youth-to-youth ministry. Take such a request, or any of your own choosing, and put it in the form of a letter. Copy it and present it to the youth group for their answers.

If the case is an actual one, take care to fictionalize it to hide the identity of the person seeking help. You don't want kids playing a guessing game as to who the mystery person is. Make every effort to protect the identity of any actual person(s) involved.

After giving the letter to the group, read it aloud and discuss the problems. One approach is to break into small groups to work on answers. If it appears that the group is just swapping ignorance or a lot of head knowledge, redirect discussion by asking questions like, "Why do you think that?" or "How would Christ respond?" Also emphasize the practical by asking, "What things have you found to work in such situations?" Be careful to stimulate up-to-date and down-to-earth responses.

Use the following letter as a guide for writing your own, or you could use it as it stands. Write it to sound as "real" as possible. That way kids are more serious about helping out with some good advice.

Dear _____:

How are you doing? You know I have been having problems at home, and I value your opinion more than anyone else's. I know that if I give you a problem to solve or whatever, you will look at it objectively. I think that is real good.

First of all, my parents tend to put their beliefs, convictions, or whatever on me. I know they've experienced some things that I haven't and that I never may, but I feel that they are sheltering me too much. For example, no guy is allowed over here if they aren't here at home. This insults me and also hurts me (let alone annoys me). It insults me because it infers they don't have faith in the type of people I choose for friends. Whenever I ask them about it they always say, "What will people say?" or "What will the neighbors think?" or else "We are only trying to protect you from a bad situation." Those are exact quotes.

Now, I understand that I am their daughter and that they are responsible for me, but why do they have to carry it so far? I'd like to know what they are going to do in a year when I have my own apartment and I can do whatever I please.

People tell me to grin and bear it a year longer, but I live right now, not in the future, and I don't care to live under such circumstances. I'm not saying I don't have freedom, because I have some—like I drive the car to school every day But Dad uses that as a string to get me to do what he wants. It's like a threat every time I don't do what he wants.

I guess what I am asking for is advice on how I can think for myself and not have to be protected. One of the last things that happened was this Sunday. I told them that they didn't have to worry about trusting me, because I didn't ever try to cover up anything from them. I told them that I have smoked and drank and smoked dope. Then they thought I was some sinner and that I needed to become closer to God. They kept me up till midnight preaching at me and telling me how bad I was.

First of all, I'll tell you my feeling on smoking, etc. I think smoking cigarettes is bad for a person, and it's a habit I hope I never have and, no, I don't smoke. I've tried it, and I didn't think it was too cool.

I drink every now and then, and I don't feel it is wrong for me. What I think would be wrong is for me to get drunk. That is one thing I just don't dig—I can't see having a hangover and everything else that goes along with it.

I guess you could call me a social drinker. I'll have a beer or whatever if I am out with kids, but I very seldom do—like maybe one or two times a month. In essence I feel drinking is fine, with moderation. But what about reputation?

Smoking dope is a constant front to me. Kids are always doing it, and I say no. I've smoked it more than once, but it didn't affect me. It was just like smoking hot air. The last time I did was last summer and I haven't since. I don't know if grass is right or wrong. That is just one thing I can't decide on. I don't really care, because if I want to smoke it I can and if I don't want to, then I won't. I'm not planning on it. It doesn't turn me on—neither does it turn me off.

Could you give me your views on the three previous things, and also give me some advice on how I can get along better with my parents?

You are probably wondering about my Christian life. Well, I know God is there, and if I want him I can get him. I try to read my Bible in the morning and at night sometimes. I fail because I am tired or in a hurry. Praying is a struggle for me because I have not found any effective way to communicate with God and Christ. Sometimes I wonder if I love God. I know the Bible says, "If you love me, you will keep my commandments," but what are they? I really would like to have a personal relationship with God, but I'm not sure how, and if I did know how, I don't know if I would be willing to put out the effort. Maybe you could advise me on this also. I would appreciate it greatly.

Well, I guess the last topic of discussion is Steve. He comes and sees me every Saturday. This weekend he is taking me down to ___ to meet his parents. I really like him a lot—more than just a friend. I don't want to end this relationship ever and neither does he. It's a type of agreement between Steve and I. I someday want to marry him if things work out the way they have been. Both of us feel the same way about it, and we are willing to wait for things to work out the way that is best, which wouldn't be until after we both graduate this year. If you would, please pray that I can be open minded about this and will do what is best from God's point of view.

I hope this letter hasn't been too exhausting. If you could, please answer me promptly. I realize you have other things to do besides answer letters, but I would be happy if you could give this some special thought and consideration. However, I will understand if you can't because you are so busy. Thanks for your time and trouble. Hope to hear from you soon.

Your friend,
Jan

The Cools and the Nerds

Conformity, popularity, acceptance, and peer pressure—your kids need to talk about these ideas in a fun and creative way. To do that divide into two groups, including in each group at least one student who can draw or sketch. Once the groups are settled at separate tables with a drawing pad and marking pens, tell one group that they are the "Cools" and the other group that they are the "Nerds." Ask the Cools draw a picture of someone who is really cool—a stereotype of everything that is currently in. Ask the Nerds to draw a picture of someone who is totally out of it—a nerd.

Post completed pictures for judging by an impartial jury (sponsors, maybe) on the basis of accuracy, humor, creativity, etc. List on the blackboard or on poster board some characteristics of a cool person and a nerdy person. See the side bar for some examples.

Next, discuss the following questions, or other questions of your choice:

1. What is the coolest thing you ever did? The nerdiest?

2. Why are items on the cool list and not the other list accepted by the crowd? What's wrong with the things on the nerdy list?

3. What's wrong with the cool list?

4. What do we want to be cool? Why is it so important?

5. Is conformity good or bad? Always

Cool	Nerdy
Not taking school work home	Wearing rain boots to school
Wearing a game jersey	Girls carrying a purse
Sports	Guys carrying a briefcase
Owning a car	Going to church or Sunday School
Cutting class	Dressing up
Smoking, drinking	Being driven by parents on a date
Dating	Bringing lunch in a lunch pail
Swearing	Golf
Eating junk food for lunch	

good or always bad?

6. What are the dangers of conformity?

7. Where do you find the most pressure to conform?

8. What does the Bible say about conformity? What does it mean?

Wrap up the discussion with some thoughts from Scripture, using passages such as Romans 12:1-2, which deal with conformity. Illustrate the concept of standing alone with heroes of the faith (such as Noah) who had to take a lot of ridicule from the crowd, but knew that they were right. The supreme example, of course, was Jesus. John 7:5 says that even his brothers rejected him. Encourage your young people to pinpoint one problem area where they can begin to break away from the crowd a little bit and live for Christ's approval, not the world's.

PROBLEMS The Secret

In this role play, Mr. and Mrs. Benjamin are close friends with Bob and Lisa Sanders. Both couples are long-time members of the same church, pastored by Rev. Evans.

Mr. and Mrs. Sanders and Rev. and Mrs. Evans are having dinner at the Benjamin's house Saturday night. A few days before the dinner, while Mrs. Benjamin is out shopping, she notices a commotion at the exit. Apparently someone is being stopped for shoplifting. To Mrs. Benjamin's amazement that someone is Lisa Sanders. Shocked and embarrassed, Mrs. Benjamin darts out of the store not knowing whether Lisa saw her or not.

Mrs. Benjamin feels very close to Lisa and plans to discuss the matter privately with her. But she is worried that such a discussion might damage their relationship.

Mr. Benjamin does not think his wife should mention it and believes it should be forgotten.

Bob Sanders has no idea his wife is shoplifting. The knowledge of it would humiliate him, and he would have a difficult time understanding or forgiving.

Lisa Sanders knows that Mrs. Benjamin saw her and wants desperately to get help from her friends but is afraid her husband, Bob, could not handle it.

Rev. Evans is totally unaware of Lisa Sanders' problem.

Mrs. Evans has a difficult time

accepting that Christians sin—especially a sin like shoplifting.

The Situation: Just as the three couples sit down for dessert, the Benjamin's teenage son runs in saying loudly, "Hey, Mom, Sonny just told me that Mrs. Sanders got arrested for shoplift—" (he suddenly see Mr. and Mrs. Sanders).

Choose actors for the role play after you read the situation to the group. Let the actors respond spontaneously to the situation. When you sense the momentum of the play slowing, stop the role play and discuss what happened. Ask the role players to discuss what they were feeling, and then get comments from the group.

How Can I Help?

Because teenagers naturally spend more time talking together than they do talking to adults, it's a good idea to equip kids to help each other in a crisis. This idea may encourage better peer ministry among your students.

Here are several case studies designed to help kids think through and discuss the issues involved in helping a friend or acquaintance through a crisis. Print them up and distribute them to the kids, use an overhead projector and a transparency of the case studies, or simply read them to the group and let them respond.

Issues that should surface include these:

■ Is it best to encourage the person to talk about the problem or to try and get her mind off it?

■ Does it help people to tell them that their problems aren't nearly as bad as other people's problems?

■ When is it good to bring God's perspective into the conversation? When isn't it good?

■ What do you do when someone seems extremely depressed or suicidal?

If you are not trained as a counselor, invite a professional counselor to attend this meeting to help deal with issues like these.

Case Studies

Read each situation carefully. Consider both what has actually happened as well as how the person is reacting to what has happened. As a group, rank the responses from best to worst based on what you know about the situation. Discuss together the strengths and weaknesses of each response. Be sure that each member of your group shares in making the decisions.

Situation #1

Fourteen-year-old Susan has been your friend for a long time. You notice that she seems angry and irritable one day. You ask her what the problem is. Susan pauses for a moment before blurting out, "Mom and Dad told me last night that they're getting divorced."

Responses:

1. I'm really sorry to hear that, Susan.

2. Why are they doing that, Susan?

3. You can come and stay with me for a while.

4. I know exactly how you feel. My parents fight a lot, too.

5. [Make up your own response.]

Situation #2

Seventeen-year-old Ben is in your calculus class. You've heard through the grapevine that Ben's application to MIT has been rejected. You and Ben aren't great friends, but he has told you that he's looked forward to attending MIT since

he was a little kid. During class you notice that his eyes are kind of puffy and red, like he's been crying. You have a chance to talk to him after class.

Responses:

1. Hey, buddy, cheer up! With your grades, there are a dozen other colleges that will be excited to have you!

2. I was sorry to hear that you didn't get into MIT, Ben.

3. Ben, there's going to be a great party tonight. How about going with me?

4. It's too bad about MIT. I guess God must have some other plans for you.

5. You look kind of down today, Ben. What's the matter?

6. [Make up your own response.]

Situation #3

Sixteen-year-old Mary has a locker next to yours. Report cards came out today. You're feeling a great sense of relief over your geometry grade. Mary, however, appears very upset.

She is extremely agitated and is walking back and forth, talking to herself. You ask her what the problem is. "My grades are terrible," she replies. "There's no way I can go home with these grades. I'm really afraid of what my dad might do to me. What am I going to do?"

Responses:

1. Maybe you should just come home with me this afternoon.

2. What are you afraid of, Mary?

3. How bad were your grades?

4. Maybe you could just not tell them about the grades, or try to change them on the report card.

5. Come on, Mary. Everyone's parents get upset with grades.

6. [Make up your own response.]

Situation #4

Ted, a junior at your school, has been your best friend for as long as you can remember. He has been acting depressed lately. He's tired all the time. He doesn't want to go out and have fun with you like he used to.

You know that things are not going well with his parents, and that his girlfriend broke up with him last week. Until now you've avoided the subject, trying instead to encourage him to do fun things and cheer him up. You've just asked him what's been bothering him so much. "I really don't know," he says. "Sometimes things just seem so hopeless. Lately I'm not sure if it's all worth it."

Responses:

1. Everyone gets down sometimes, Ted. I'm sure you'll feel better soon.

2. I'll pray for you, Ted. God understands your feelings and wants to help you.

3. Maybe all you need is to get out and do some fun stuff. Let's go to the mall together and get your mind off your problems.

4. What seems so hopeless, Ted?

5. What do you mean, "I'm not sure if it's all worth it?"

6. [Make up your own response.]

Rock Talk

If you're ready to be surprised by the deep feelings and sometimes shocking political views of your students, try building a discussion around the kids' favorite music. Since often their identity is wrapped up in their songs, hearing kids talk about their music lets you know what their inner thoughts and struggles are. And a sense of community is built, too, because the kids feel the freedom to express their musical tastes without being judged or censored.

Ask your kids beforehand to bring a recording of one of their most meaningful songs. Tell them that they should be prepared to explain what they think their songs are about and why the songs means so much to them.

Meanwhile, recruit one adult discussion leader for every five students, and supply them with a tape or CD player or turntable and six copies of

these discussion questions:

1. How would you classify this song? (pop, New Wave, punk, rock, heavy metal, folk, reggae, rap, etc.)

2. What is the song about?

3. What qualities of this song make it meaningful to you? Why do you like it?

4. What do you visualize when you hear this song?

5. How could this song influence the way you think?

6. What does the design on the cassette case (or album cover) suggest?

At the meeting divide the kids into groups of five as they arrive. Then the adult discussion leaders distribute the question sheets and ask the teenagers to play their songs one at a time and answer the questions.

Top 40

For an effective discussion on the good and bad of rock music, have a "Top 40" night. Bring a selection of popular rock records and have the kids vote on the ones that they like the best, according to certain standards. You might find it worthwhile to get the words to the songs so that your kids will be able to follow along while listening. Then play the records for the kids to judge using judging sheets with the following criteria:

1. Lyrics: What is the song's message? Does it support or contradict Christian values and the Word of God?

2. The Artist: What is he or she like as a person? Is the artist a good role model for young people? Does the group avoid behavior that offends those who follow Christ?

3. Overall Effect of the Song: Does this song make you feel more positive about your faith or about life, or more negative? Does it strengthen you as a Christian or weaken you? Or is it neutral?

Before the kids rate the songs that they listen to, you should discuss each of the three criterion so that they know what each one means. You may want to add another category as well: **The Music**. In this category kids decide whether or not the record would be considered good music or not.

After the kids have rated all the songs, use the results to come up with your own youth group "Top 10" or "Top 5."

SELF Love for Others

Our love for others depends largely on what we think of ourselves; Jesus himself said to "love your neighbor as yourself." This self-concept quiz encourages your young people to understand themselves better.

Ask your kids to write on paper the first 20 things that come to their minds in answer to the question, "Who am I?" Assure them that this is private so they'll respond honestly.

Example:

I am—
- Harvey Klutz
- smart
- a son
- bald
- a Christian

Questions for discussion:

1. Must I like everything about myself in order to accept myself as God does?

2. What can I do to change what I don't like about myself?

3. How do I alter my self-concept? How do I alter what others think of me? what Christ thinks of me?

4. Do others perceive me the way I think they do?

5. Can I be confident about myself if my self-concept depends on others' opinion of me?

6. Does my self-concept depend on my roles—student, leader, child, jock, party girl, class clown?

Now ask each student to choose a partner and assess each other's self-concept—that is, student A lists what she thinks student B thinks of himself. Then ask them to compare these assessments with their written responses to the earlier "Who am I?" question.

You Are the Designer! [this is the boys' version]

Write in the blanks below how you'd design yourself if you had the power. (It's okay to be satisfied with any of your existing attributes.) When you've completed the chart, share with your group what things about yourself you'd change, what you wouldn't change, and why you chose what you did.

hair color and style
talent   weight
shoe size   height
eye color
appearance (looks like—)
clothes   build
skin color   personality
money   name

You Are the Designer! [this is the girls' version]

Write in the blanks below how you'd design yourself if you had the power. (It's okay to be satisfied with any of your existing attributes.) When you've completed the chart, share with your group what things about yourself you'd change, what you wouldn't change, and why you chose what you did.

hair color and style
talent   weight
shoe size   height
eye color
appearance (looks like—)
clothes   figure
skin color   personality
money   name

SELF-DISCLOSURE

Show and Tell

Invite your students to bring a personal object that represents something they feel about life—trophies, books, pictures, mementoes, etc. After all explain what feelings lay behind the objects they brought, then permit questions. When the kids are finished asking and answering, ask, "What new things did you learn about those who shared? What did you learn about yourselves?"

Newsstand

If you're looking for a way to encourage honest self-expression among your students, try this activity that allows kids to identify themselves with a popular magazine.

Randomly divide the large group into small discussion groups of four to six people. Choose magazines from the list of magazines below and bring enough copies of different issues to give a copy of a magazine to each person. After giving the kids a few minutes to browse and trade magazines among themselves, lead them to discuss the three following questions one at a time. Anyone may pass if they wish.

1. Which magazine(s) best describes you right now? Explain Why. Which magazine(s) best describes the way you would like to be?

2. Due to a sudden paper shortage, the government will only permit publication of three magazines chosen by a majority of the people. Which ones will you vote for?

3. If you had one full page in any magazine to do with as you wished, how would you use it? What would you put on the page, and in what magazine would it appear?

Allow ample time after each question for everyone to respond. Remember that in a discussion such as this, there are no right or wrong answers.

The 30 popular magazines listed below are found on most newsstands and reflect a wide range of interests. Add your favorites and delete those you'd rather not use.

1. Rolling Stone	16. Better Homes and
2. TV Guide	Gardens
3. Ladies' Home Journal	17. Parents
4. Self	18. Playgirl
5. Psychology Today	19. Esquire
6. Surfer	20. Police Gazette
7. Time	21. Consumer Reports
8. Playboy	22. Ms.
9. Seventeen	23. New Yorker
10. Sports Illustrated	24. Glamour
11. Reader's Digest	25. National Geographic
12. Mad	26. Hollywood Reporter
13. Thrasher	27. Decision
14. Intellectual Digest	28. Wrestling!
15. U.S. News & World	29. National Enquirer
Report	30. People

Ways To Serve God

SERVING GOD

To start your youth group thinking about how to put their faith into action, hand out the following list of 10 statements for them to circle "T" for true and "F" for false.

After briefly discussing their answers in the large group, they can explore the subject in more depth in small groups, brainstorming one of these five topics in each group: Ways to serve God in 1) our personal lives; 2) our families; 3) our church; 4) our

Ways To Serve God

T F 1. The only way to serve God is to be a pastor.
T F 2. You cannot serve God at school.
T F 3. If you're being paid for a job, it can't be service to God.
T F 4. Only certain people can serve God.
T F 5. We should serve God only on Sundays.
T F 6. Feeding ducks is serving God.
T F 7. Serving God may require a sacrifice.
T F 8. Men serve God better than women.
T F 9. Driving the church van is serving God.
T F 10. Getting good grades has nothing to do with serving God.

community; 5) the world. As each group's spokesperson reports her group's ideas to the entire group, compile a list (to print up for the next meeting) of ways the kids can serve God.

SEXUALITY   Male and Female

What does it mean to be a man? What does it mean to be a woman? What does God have to say about the whole issue of men's and women's roles? Guide your kids to begin to answer these questions for themselves by asking them to answer and discuss the following questionnaire:

1. What does it mean to be female? (Or what does it bring to your mind?)

2. What does it mean to be male? (Or what does it bring to your mind?)

3. Girls: I feel most feminine when...

Guys: I feel most masculine when...

4. I think a man/woman feels most masculine/feminine when...(describe how you think the opposite sex feels)

5. List a few personality differences between men and women. What generalizations can you make?

Summarize what you as the leader hear the group saying: the main points and any similarities or differences between the way the girls answered the questionnaire and the way the guys did.

Then ask several readers to read aloud Genesis 1:27-28, 2:18-25; Galatians 3:26-29; and Philippians 2:1-8. In light of the Scripture, discuss the following questions:

1. Why do you think God made different sexes?

2. What do you think God's attitude toward men and women was then (and is now)?

3. What are some of the good things about the differences between the sexes?

4. Based on the passages in Galatians and Philippians, how should Christians view the sexes? Is one superior to the other? How do they complement each other? How should we treat each other as a result?

Conclude by asking the students to think of specific things they could do to understand the opposite sex better—things like learning more about the types of things the opposite sex is interested in, stopping to think the next time they are about to make a disrespectful or prejudicial comment, or becoming aware of how they may have locked themselves and others into certain roles, ignoring the unity we have in Christ.

Spiritual-Growth Chart

SPIRITUAL GROWTH

Here's a creative way to get your kids to think and talk about spiritual growth and to evaluate their own walk with God. Using paper and pencil, your kids create a chart representing the last two years of their lives, labeling the months and years on a time line. Ask them to chart their spiritual ups and downs on the time line. Any marks above the time line represent a period of growth, any marks below the line indicate decline, and any mark along the line represents no change in their spiritual progress.

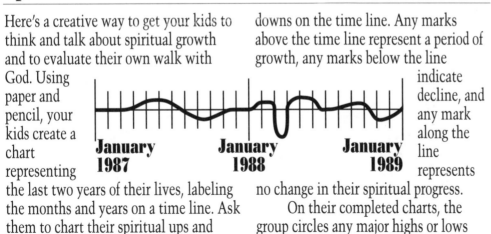

On their completed charts, the group circles any major highs or lows and any extended period of no change, and on the back of the chart they write down why that condition existed. Discuss these findings together, using questions like, What causes growth in our spiritual lives? Is there anything wrong with a chart that looks like a roller coaster? What have we learned about ourselves from these charts?

After the discussion, chart the spiritual progress of some colorful characters in the Bible. The up and down character of David's experiences of believing God, for example, encourages the kids to view their charts as normal and acceptable and their ups and downs as part of the process of living in relationship to God.

STEALING The Food Store Robbery

The following story, centered around a man who steals to care for his family, rouses kids to discuss not only stealing but also the corporate structure, family stress, justice, and law and order.

Tell the story and use the questions that follow to start the group talking. To keep the details of the story straight, each student may need a copy of the story to refer to. Answers to the complex problems the story presents are not clear-cut. Instead it is the struggle to propose solutions that causes growth in the kids.

The Story

The automobile factory where Ed has worked for the past 10 years is

experiencing hard times, and the plant managers must lay off a number of employees. Ed's plant manager has always worried that Ed might get his job, so to protect himself, he lays Ed off.

Ed can't find a job anywhere. After 18 months of unsuccessful job hunting, his unemployment payments run out, and Ed is forced to sell his insurance so his family can have food and make the house payments. When that money runs out, Ed and Hilda discuss the possibility of applying for welfare. Hilda will not hear of it. She considers it degrading and a sign of failure. In fact, Hilda considers Ed a failure and constantly nags him to do something about their situation. She threatens to leave him.

One evening, despite many warnings to stay out of the street, one of Ed's children runs into the street after his soccer ball. A stolen car driven by a 19-year-old runaway runs into Ed's child, seriously injuring him. The child requires hospitalization and the bills will be enormous. Of course, the runaway has no insurance.

In desperation Ed applies for a loan from his bank. Ed has good credit, but the banker refuses the loan. (The banker has involved the bank's money in some questionable investments that have overextended the bank's loan limit.)

When Ed explains the situation to Hilda, she explodes into a hysterical rage and threatens to leave. She calls Ed a failure and a no-good who doesn't care about his child or his wife. She tells him he'd better be gone when she returns and stomps out of the house. Distraught and confused, Ed robs the local food store. When his wife returns, Ed shows her the money and explains that a close friend loaned it to them. They use the money to purchase food and clothing for the children, but within a day Ed is arrested by the police. He explains, "All I wanted to do was feed my family."

After conferring with the city officials, the prosecutor suggest dropping the case, if Ed will pay back the money and seek counseling with the welfare department. But the store owner is a strong law and order advocate and refuses to drop the charges. He believes that Ed is a thief and ought to be punished. Ed is forced to go to trial where he pleads guilty and is sentenced by the judge.

Questions for discussion:

1. Which person was most responsible for the robbery of the food store? Rank the characters from most responsible to least responsible. Give reasons for the order that you choose.

   The husband, Ed
   The injured child
   The teenage driver
   The wife, Hilda
   The plant manager
   The banker
   The food store owner

2. Was Ed wrong to rob the food store? Why or why not?

3. Hilda was certainly a nagging wife, but didn't she have something to nag about? Do you feel any compassion for Hilda? If so, why?

4. Do you agree with Hilda's refusal to accept welfare?

5. What do you think Hilda did after Ed was arrested? What should she have done?

6. If you were the food store owner, would you have pressed charges?

7. If you were the judge at the trial where Ed confessed to the crime, what sentence would you hand down?

8. Which person was the worst? Which was the best? Why?

9. What is your concept of justice?

TELEVISION   TV or No TV

The best way to use the following questionnaire on TV watching is divide the group into groups of three kids who fill it out as a unit. Then bring the whole group together to discuss conclusions.

1. How many hours a week do you watch TV? (Average the time.)

2. What's one program you watch each week? (List one for each member.)

3. List three things you think have shaped your life and determined your values more than TV. List three that have had less influence.

4. List at least five ways TV has changed our society and affected our views of ourselves, others, and things.

5. Rate each of the items you listed in question four as "basically good," "basically bad," "neutral," or "questionable."

6. In what area of your life has TV most affected you?

7. If there were no TV, how would your life be different? What would you do without TV?

8. What guidelines does the Bible give that can apply to your television viewing? Try to come up with several.

9. Could watching TV ever be considered a sin? If so, when?

10. How can a person set guidelines for his own viewing? Write three rules for TV viewers that you think would generally be helpful for most everyone.

Back Rubs and The Gospel

TOUCHING

Here is fun way to help people to experience touching and community in a safe and non-threatening atmosphere. (It feels good, too.) Each person is to give to receive back rubs according to the following list, which should be printed up so that everyone has a copy. Following the "back-rubbing" period (10-15 minutes) follow up with a discussion. Some discussion question are provided.
Rules:

1. The giver will be scored by the receiver on a scale of 1 to 10 with 10 being best.

2. On your sheet, the score is automatically 5 points for any back rub received by you.

3. You will receive a score from 1 to 10 only on back rubs which you give. The receiver will judge your back rub.

4. No score is valid without the initials of the other person (giver or receiver).

5. You may not refuse to give or receive a back rub if someone asks you.

6. The same person may be used only twice, once giving and once receiving.

7. The highest score at the end of the time limit wins.

The Back Rubs:	SCORE	INITIAL
1. Give to someone taller.		
2. Receive from someone shorter.		
3. Give to someone older.		
4. Receive from someone younger.		
5. Give to someone of the opposite sex.		
6. Receive from someone of the same sex.		
7. Give to someone with shoes on.		
8. Receive from someone without shoes on.		
9. Give to someone with blue eyes.		
10. Receive from someone with brown eyes.		
11. Give to someone wearing red.		
12. Receive from someone wearing green.		
13. Give to someone who lives less than one mile from you.		
14. Receive from someone who lives more than one mile from you.		
15. Give to someone who wears glasses or contacts.		
16. Receive from someone who doesn't wear glasses or contacts.		
17. Give to someone with an even numbered address.		
18. Receive from someone with an even address.		
19. Give to someone whose last initial is before yours in the alphabet.		
20. Receive from someone whose last initial comes after yours in the alphabet.		

Questions for discussion:

1. What are some feelings you had? Were you embarrassed?

2. Those who did both, did you like giving or receiving better?

3. Has this experience affected your feelings in any way with the rest of the group?

4. What can we learn about Christian love from this experience?

TOUGH ISSUES   Agree/Disagree

For this discussion starter, give groups of three a list of statements like those below. One person in each group reads a statement from the list. After allowing themselves 30 seconds to consider their response to the statement, they simultaneously indicate by holding up a number of fingers how strongly they agree or disagree with the statement. Ten fingers indicate total agreement, and 1 finger indicates total disagreement.

If the number of fingers are within two of each other, the group doesn't need to discuss the issue (unless they want to). If their numbers are more than two from each other, then they must talk over their opinions with each other. After 30 minutes or so, come back together as a total group and discuss the statements that generated the most discussion and those that evoked the widest differences of opinion.

Some sample statements:

1. I would leave a party shortly after arriving if I were not having a good time.

2. I would discuss my personal family problems with friends.

3. There are some crimes for which the death penalty should apply.

4. If I were offered a less satisfying job at a 25% increase in salary, I would take it.

5. Parents should stay away from a long-awaited party to attend a sick child.

6. I could forgive and forget if my mate were unfaithful.

7. Doing the laundry is woman's work.

8. Any teenager who wants birth control

should be allowed to get it with no hassle.

9. I would ask a friend to stop smoking around me if the smoke bothered me.

10. A parent should immediately defend a child if the other parent is punishing him unfairly.

11. There should be no secrets between good friends.

12. The housework that women do is usually taken for granted by the males who live in the house.

13. Schools should teach sex education as early as kindergarten.

14. Churches should teach sex education.

15. Children should be spanked for some types of misbehavior.

16. If a man enjoys housework and a woman enjoys a career, they should

pursue these roles.

17. It is a mother's and father's duty to attend school functions in which their child participates.

18. It is important to remember birthdays of family and friends.

19. It's okay for a 13-year-old to see an R-rated movie.

20. Women with small children should not work unless it's a financial necessity.

21. Marijuana should be legalized.

22. Kids should not have to account for their allowance.

23. Parents should regulate how much TV a 10-year-old kid can watch.

24. Schools should quit using grades to evaluate students.

25. I would say something if I saw a friend littering.

The Island Affair

VALUES

As your young people discuss this story, they will discover—in a non-threatening setting—what it is they believe and value

Use the diagram below while telling the story.

The two circles represent two islands surrounded by shark-infested waters. A nearby shipwreck leaves only five survivors, who manage to reach the safety of the islands. Albert is separated from his fiancee, Carla. Carla is stranded on the other island with her mother Della. Bruno, a young man of about the

same age as Albert, ends up on Albert's island. The fifth survivor is an older man, Edgar. He is a loner, but is stranded on the same island with Carla and Della.

The situation is this: Albert and Carla are deeply in love and engaged to be married. After two months of being separated and yet in sight of each other, Carla becomes despondent. One day while walking around the island, Carla discovers a crude boat hollowed out of an old tree. It looks seaworthy. Then Edgar appears. He has just finished making the boat. Carla explains her longing to reach the other island and Albert and pleads with Edgar to let her have the boat. Edgar refuses saying the

boat was made for his escape not hers. After continued pleading by Carla, Edgar makes a proposal. If Carla will make love to him, he will take her to the other island in his boat. Carla asks for time to think about it and runs to find her mother, Della. She explains to her mother that rescue looks hopeless and that if they are to be stranded on an island, she should at least be with the one she loves. Della listens with understanding, and after much thought gives her advice. "I know you sincerely love Albert, and I understand your desire to be with him. But I'm afraid the cost is too high. You will do what you want, but my advice is to wait a bit longer. I'm sure a better solution will come, and you will be glad you waited."

Carla considers her mother's advice for a number of days. She decides, however, to accept Edgar's offer. Carla makes love to Edgar. Edgar keeps his part of the bargain and rows Carla to Albert's island. Albert and Carla embrace and are very happy. But during the day's conversation, Carla recounts for Albert the bargain she struck with Edgar. She confesses that she made love to Edgar, but only because she loves Albert so much.

Albert is deeply hurt. He tries to

understand, but after long discussion and thought he tells Carla that although he loves her very much, he cannot continue their relationship knowing that she made love to another man. Carla tries to change Albert's mind, but to no avail.

While this discussion is going on, Bruno is listening from behind some bushes. When Albert leaves, Bruno comes to Carla and explains that he thinks what she did was admirable. He understands that her experience with Edgar was the result of desperation and was an act of love for Albert. Bruno tells Carla that he would readily accept someone who would pay such a high price for love, and he would be willing to care for Carla in spite of what Albert did. Carla accepts.

Give each person in the group paper and pencil to rank the characters in the story from best to worst. Then break into small groups and ask the groups to agree on a choice for best person and worst person. Return to the large groups to hear how the other small groups chose and the reasons for their choices.

Use the following questions for further discussion:

Carla:

1. Was she justified in what she did to be with Albert?

2. Should she have accepted Bruno's proposal?

3. What should happen to her?

Albert:

1. Should he have accepted Carla?

2. If you were Albert, what would have done? Why?

4. If Albert were a Christian, would he have behaved differently? If so, how?

Della:

1. Was her advice acceptable? If not, what advice would you have given?

2. How would you treat Carla after she chose not to listen to you?

Edgar:

1. Is there any justification for his action?

2. If you were Della, and were stuck on an island with Edgar, what would you do? Why?

3. What would you do if Edgar asked you to forgive him?

Bruno:

1. Why do you think he accepted Carla?

2. Would you have accepted her? Why or why not?

Life Auction

Divide your group into small groups and give each group a sheet like the one below. After each group finishes its sheet, bidding begins. After the auction is over, the whole group then discusses and evaluates what happened. The items below could be changed and adapted to fit your particular group.

Life Auction

You have received $5,000 and can spend the money any way you desire. Budget the money in the column labeled "Amount Budgeted." We will auction off each item—the item going to the highest bidder. Your goal to gain the things you most desire.

	AMOUNT BUDGETED	AMOUNT SPENT	HIGHEST BID
1. A wonderful family life without any hassles.			
2. All the money I need to be happy.			
3. Never to be sick.			
4. To find the right mate, one who is good-looking and fulfills me.			
5. Never to have pimples.			
6. To be able to do whatever I want when I want.			
7. To have all the power the President has.			
8. To be the best-looking person.			
9. To have a real hunger to read the Bible.			
10. To be able to understand all things.			
11. To eliminate all hunger and disease in the world.			
12. To always be close to God.			
13. Never to feel lonely or put down.			
14. Always be happy and peaceful.			
15. Never feel hurt.			
16. To own a beautiful home, car, boat, plane, and seven motorcycles— one for each day of the week.			
17. To be super smart without ever having to attend school.			
18. To be able to be superior in all things.			
19. To be filled with God's presence in the most dynamic way.			
20. To always know that I am in God's will.			
21. To be the greatest athlete in the world.			
22. To be looked up to by everyone else.			
23. To become a star on "Star Trek, the Next Generation."			
24. To always have a lot of close friends who never let me down.			
25. To walk close to God.			

Time Machine

Discussing the following story reveals to kids what they value in a person as well as forces them to talk through disagreement to come to a group consensus.

There is about to be a nuclear holocaust. The human race as we know it will be totally wiped out. However, 10 people have discovered a way to survive by getting into a time machine, which will take them into the future, where they can start the human race all over again. The ten people are:

1. An accountant
2. His pregnant wife
3. A liberal arts coed
4. A pro basketball player
5. An intelligent female movie star
6. A black medical student
7. A famous novelist
8. A biochemist
9. A 70-year-old clergyman
10. An armed policeman

Unfortunately, at the last minute, it is discovered that the machine will only take six people instead of the original ten. Your group's job is to decide which six will be saved and which four must die. You have 30 minutes in which to decide.

Disregarding the technicalities of the story, each small group of four or five is to choose the six people they feel should go in the time machine. At the end of the time period, the groups discuss their choices with the entire group.

After each group shares its selections, ask questions for further discussion: How did your group get along during the process of making a decision? Did you listen to each other, or were you so stubborn that no progress was made? Did you feel that no one would listen to you? Did you feel that you had the right answers? Are there in fact any right answers? What do your selections teach you about your values?

Value Teasers

Here are stories to help your youth group members find out what they value.

The Talking Friend

You and a good friend of yours are equally unprepared for a test. Together you cheat and pass. Your friend, however, begins to feel guilty about it and confesses to the teacher. In the process your friend implicates you as well, and you both automatically fail the test.

1. Should the friend have confessed?

2. Couldn't the friend just have confessed to God and not the teacher?

3. Should the friend have told the teacher about you?

4. What things should you say to your friend?

5. Is it okay to cheat, knowing that God will forgive you if you ask him to?

The Borrowing Brother

You and your brother share the same bedroom. You have made it very clear to your brother, however, that he is to leave your belongings alone. You have a large CD collection and a CD system that you purchased with your own money.

You come home from school one day and find many of your best CD's all over your room...your favorite CD is destroyed. You blow up at your brother, and he apologizes and offers to buy a new CD...but you're still furious. You threaten to tell your parents about it and refuse to accept his apology. You tell him to get out of your room. Finally, he has had enough and says to you, "I know that you've been seeing Linda, even though Mom and Dad told you not to. You've been telling the folks that you get off work at ten, but you really get off at nine. And if you keep yelling at me and threatening me, I'm going to tell them what I know."

1. What's wrong with not wanting to let others use valuable possessions that might be wrecked?

2. Which person in this situation is the worst in your opinion? Why?

3. Is blackmail wrong?

4. What would you do?

The Changing Parents

One evening a couple of your friends come by, and you decide to attend a movie the next weekend. You ask your parents who, although they've never heard of the movie, give their permission. The next Friday night your friends come to the house to pick you up, and your folks ask where you are going. You remind them that they had given you permission to go to a movie. Your dad responds, "Well, I did some checking, and I was going to talk to you. I forgot you were going tonight. But the movie, from what my friends tell me, is no good. It contains profanity and explicit sex, so I don't want you to see it. Sorry, but you can't go."

Your friends look at each other with shock and amazement. They can't believe it. As you watch them leave, you see them smile at each other like they think your folks are real losers. You are embarrassed, humiliated, and angry.

1. Did the parents do the right thing?

2. Do parents have the right to change their minds at the last minute?

3. If you were a parent, how would you have handled the situation?

4. If your parents reacted like the parents in the story, how would you respond?

Broken Banana

Here's a way to help your youth group talk about vulnerability. This discussion helps kids see that, in order for people to really get to know them, they must "peel off" their outer skin.

Ahead of time buy three bananas. Bruise one banana in such a way that the insides are brown, but the outside doesn't show it. Slice the second banana in several places without peeling it. Here's how to do it:

Take the needle and thread and

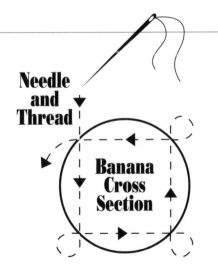

Needle and Thread

Banana Cross Section

the banana as shown in the diagram. Then grab both ends of the thread and pull. This will slice the banana inside without damaging the skin. Do this in several places.

At the meeting ask the kids to describe the three bananas: How do they look the same, and how do they look different? Peel the banana that has not been tampered with. Describe how good it looks, how fresh and wholesome it is. Then peel the smashed up, bruised banana and ask the kids to describe it for you. The inside will be mushy, dark, and rotten. As you peel the third banana, the sliced sections will fall off. The kids will be amazed at how you were able to slice it without slicing the skin.

Questions for discussion:

1. How are the bananas like people?

2. How can we really get to know people?

3. What must you do for people to know the real you?

4. How can you help a person who is hurting inside?

5. How is being vulnerable important for good relationships?

WISDOM   Wisdom Test

This discussion starter based on Proverb 7—9 stimulates discussion on wisdom. Give each of the kids a copy of the following survey and ask them to choose one answer for each statement. After they have completed it, discuss each of the questions in depth.

1. My friends and family generally consider me to be...
   a. a foolish person
   b. lacking common sense
   c. a "wise guy"
   d. able to make fairly wise decisions, except when it comes to _____
   e. wiser than most people
   f. one of the wisest people in the world
   g. other: _____

2. I consider myself to be...
   a. a foolish person
   b. lacking common sense
   c. a "wise guy"

d. able to make fairly wise decisions, except when it comes to_____
e. wiser than most people
f. one of the wisest people in the world
g. other: _____

3. I can be talked into things...
   a. always or almost always
   b. often, even when I know it's a foolish decision
   c. only when I really wanted to be in the first place
   d. sometimes when I see new information
   e. only when physical violence accompanies talk
   f. never
   g. other: _____

4. My wisest actions have...
   a. resulted in benefits even others can see
   b. brought about changes only I can appreciate
   c. are still foolish when compared with the actions of most people
   d. are just about like everyone's wisest actions
   e. are wiser than those of anyone else I know
   f. other: _____

5. When I'm criticized, I generally...
   a. punch out the person who criticized me

b. react by screaming and/or yelling
c. pout and try to make the person who criticized me feel guilty
d. ignore the criticism
e. try to honestly evaluate the criticism and change my ways if I feel it is warranted
f. appreciate the person who had the guts to share with me and tell her so
g. other: _____

6. One area where I generally show wisdom in my life is...
   a. money/finances
   b. God
   c. friendships
   d. sex
   e. family
   f. use of time/scheduling
   g. food
   h. other: _____

7. One area where I rarely show wisdom and in which I need drastic improvement is...
   a. money/finances
   b. God
   c. friendships
   d. sex
   e. family
   f. use of time/scheduling
   g. food
   h. other: _____

WORK   The Christian and Work

Rate the following statements on a scale of one to five according to whether or not you agree with them. Five is high (strongly agree), three is neutral, and one is low (strongly disagree)

____ a. The most important thing is for the worker to keep his job at all costs, even if he has to do things that are against his conscience.

____ b. If a worker is paid for 40 hours a week, but he can accomplish the same work in 30, he has an obligation to inform his employer that he is being paid for 10 hours during which he does not really work.

____ c. If a worker sees a fellow worker not doing his work, it is her responsibility to report this to the supervisor.

____ d. There is nothing wrong with taking paper, pens, and other small items from work for use at home.

____ e. There is nothing wrong with trying to please the boss in order to get a promotion.

____ f. All persons have an obligation to use their talents to the fullest extent.

____ g. Workers have the right to strike.

____ h. Workers should belong to unions.

____ i. There is nothing wrong with taking extra time for lunch or leaving work early if the assigned work is completed.

____ j. Workers on one shift should accomplish as much as those on any other shift.

What do we mean by the statement "an honest day's work for an honest day's pay"?

Does the Christian have any obligations to his fellow workers in regard to the way in which he does his work?

What, Me Worry?

Worry is something we all do. The following is a stimulating outline for a discussion on worry.

1. Respond to these statements:
   a. Christians should never worry.
   b. Why worry?
   c. If you don't care enough to worry, you don't care.

2. List some things that you worry about.

3. List some things that your parents worry about.

4. List good consequences of worrying.

5. List bad consequences of worrying.

6. What would you say to someone who was worried about:
   a. their parents getting a divorce.
   b. failing in school.
   c. unconfessed sin.
   d. the recent loss of a boyfriend or girlfriend.
   e. future plans.
   f. a bad case of acne.
   g. a meaningless prayer life.
   h. a recent failure.
   i. death.
   j. being pregnant and unmarried.

Youth and the Church

Type the following "Youth and the Church" survey, and give copies to each person in your group. Ask your kids to invite adults in the church to complete the survey.

Youth and the Church Survey
Answer each question briefly and honestly. Say what you really believe. If you have no children of school age, answer on the basis of what you know about teenagers from your contacts with them. Do not put your name on this sheet.

1. What do you see as the role and relevancy of the church for today's youth?

2. What things do young people like about church? dislike?

3. How meaningful and relevant is it to them?

4. My children attend church school, church, and/or youth groups (or don't attend) because...

5. My children's friends attend (or don't attend) because...

6. My children's biggest gripe about church activities is...

7. What's one thing you'd change about how the church relates to its young people?

8. How can young people become more a part of the church?

Bring the survey to the next meeting, read the answers out loud, and discuss things your youth group can do to help the church become more meaningful for its young people.

Youth Group Hand to Hand

Get your young people to think and talk about the youth group with this discussion starter. Have each person trace his hand on a piece of typing paper. Then, using each finger and the palm as a place to sketch, ask the kids to draw the following with paints, pens, or markers.

Finger 1: Symbolize something your youth group has done for others in the past.

Finger 2: Symbolize the purpose of our youth group.

Finger 3: Draw the most important activity of our youth group.

Finger 4: Draw a picture of our youth group's greatest achievement last year.

Thumb: Symbolize what you feel the goal of our group should be.

Palm: Write three words that should be most important to our group.

Once everyone has finished sketching their hands, ask them to explain their sketches, one finger at a time. Before they leave, ask your group members to cut out their hands and tape them hand to hand around the room.